Once Upon A Dream

Midnight Melodies

Edited By Byron Tobolik

First published in Great Britain in 2024 by:

YoungWriters
Est. 1991

Young Writers
Remus House
Coltsfoot Drive
Peterborough
PE2 9BF
Telephone: 01733 890066
Website: www.youngwriters.co.uk

All Rights Reserved
Book Design by Ashley Janson
© Copyright Contributors 2024
Softback ISBN 978-1-83565-589-4
Printed and bound in the UK by BookPrintingUK
Website: www.bookprintinguk.com
YB0598F

FOREWORD

Welcome Reader, to a world of dreams.

For Young Writers' latest competition, we asked our writers to dig deep into their imagination and create a poem that paints a picture of what they dream of, whether it's a make-believe world full of wonder or their aspirations for the future.

The result is this collection of fantastic poetic verse that covers a whole host of different topics. Let your mind fly away with the fairies to explore the sweet joy of candy lands, join in with a game of fantasy football, or you may even catch a glimpse of a unicorn or another mythical creature. Beware though, because even dreamland has dark corners, so you may turn a page and walk into a nightmare!

Whereas the majority of our writers chose to stick to a free verse style, others gave themselves the challenge of other techniques such as acrostics and rhyming couplets.

Each piece in this collection shows the writers' dedication and imagination – we truly believe that seeing their work in print gives them a well-deserved boost of pride, and inspires them to keep writing, so we hope to see more of their work in the future!

CONTENTS

Acres Hill Community Primary School, Sheffield

Amy Abid (10)	1
Lana Khawaja (10)	2
Lucas Wright (10)	4

Adel Primary School, Adel

Aayan Sharma (11)	6
Jovan Lota (11)	8
Diyor Aliev (10)	9
Nellie Gordon (10)	10
Nayan Edwards (11)	11
Liya Shahid (11)	12
Elise Mackay (10)	13
Alex Vulcu (10)	14
George Dickinson (11)	15
Maryam Shah (11)	16
Aris Padfield (11)	17
Noah Vigar (11)	18
Nikolas Savic (11)	19
Gurnek Bhogal (11)	20
Naail Akbar (10)	21
Jordan Reid (10)	22
Caitlin Smith (11)	23
Okan Dervish (10)	24
Leah Mackay (10)	25
Harpreet Virdee (10)	26

Bempton Primary School, Bempton

Daisy Swales (9)	27
Louis Robson (8)	28
Elizabeth Hakner (8)	29

Ezri Wilson (7)	30
Isabelle Butler (7)	31
Charlie Hickie (9)	32
Harvey Lord (7)	33
Ines Braithwate (9)	34
Faris Watti (8)	35
Maxi J (6)	36
Josie Noble (9)	37
Rory Hutson (8)	38
Albie Warrington (9)	39
Jack Collins (8)	40
Eden Patchett (8)	41
Toby Hogg (8)	42
Olivia Colman (8)	43
Chester Barker (8)	44
Jonathan Grouse (8)	45

Clements Primary Academy, Haverhill

Maddie Vaughan (10)	46
Leah Moore (10)	47
Pixie Probyn (9)	48
Bonnie Lisher (9)	49
Maria Owczarek (10)	50
Isabelle Smith (10)	51
Amberina Shahzad (10)	52
Scarlett DeCruze (9)	53
Anaya White (10)	54
Ifra Saeed (9)	55
Cian Jeffrey (9)	56
Ruvar Marume (9)	57
Stephanie Biko (10)	58
Robin Lee (9)	59
Talulah Kinsey (9)	60
Jaxson Coker (9)	61

Diogo Santos (9)	62
Aisha Barros (9)	63
Ariana Krasauskaite (9)	64
Ava Webb (9)	65
Chase Hill (9)	66
Patrick Cilheiro (9)	67
Isabella Limpus (10)	68

Egloskerry Primary School, Launceston

Jake Pugsley (11)	69
Poppy Ranson (10)	70
Aaliyah Mee (10)	72
Ellie Bloye (9)	74
Max Uglow (11)	76
Daniel Gunn (10)	77
Charlie Cox (11)	78
Harvey Blow (9)	79
Esmay Jackson (10)	80
Emilia Powell (11)	81
Leo Lawrence (11)	82
Albie Barnard (10)	83
Amelie Cox (9)	84
Sebastian Parsons (11)	85
Gregory Heywood (10)	86
Jack Cox (10)	87
Jaydan Legg (9)	88
Jack Hawkins (10)	89
Lola Gregory (10)	90
Chyanne Cathrae (10)	91
Daniel Humber (9)	92
Liam Butt (11)	93

Horton Grange Primary School, Bradford

Ajwa-Noor Zeeshan (8)	94
Rosario Urbina (7)	95
Muhammad-Musa Ali (7)	96
Maariya Bismillah (7)	97
Anisa Ahmed (7)	98
Alyaan Amran (8)	99
Emmanuel Adebambo (8)	100

Minahil Noor (8)	101

Ireleth St Peter's CE Primary School, Ireleth

Edie McDonnell (7)	102
Daisy Chapples (7)	104
Lennox Read (8)	106
Alba Dalton (8)	108
Oliver Cush (8)	109
Ellis Maiden (7)	110
Ayla Askew (7)	111
Austin Taylor (7)	112
Austin Finnie (7)	113
Florence Gardiner (7)	114
Willow Keel (8)	115
Olivia Gaskell (6)	116
Olivia Clark (8)	117
Nathan Roberts (8)	118
William Galston (7)	119
Ted Archer (7)	120
Adam Colquhoun (7)	121
Elva Dalton (7)	122
Parker Price (8)	123
Elijah Knox (6)	124
Leon Bolton (8)	125
Lachlan Roberts (8)	126
Zane Aboudi (7)	127

Jameah Girls Academy, Leicester

Aasiyah Kolia (10)	128
Amirah Osman (11)	130
Zaynab Pathan (11)	131

John Locke Academy, Uxbridge

Isabella Jaques (11)	132
Caitlin I'Anson (10)	134
Judie Atoui (11)	136
Anaaya Kale (11)	137
Tanaya Patel (10)	138
Ahana Madhok (10)	140
Vatsal Agarwal (10)	141

Asya Javadzadeh (10)	142
Amelia Kopczak-West (11)	143
Leo Curtin (10)	144
Daniel Harding (11)	145
Adam Zarouk (11)	146
Ali Khan	147
Olivia Arlauskaite (10)	148
Joanna Buaron (11)	149
Varnika Badarla (11)	150
Sebastian Feneck (10)	151

Lyndhurst School, Camberley

Naik Kalkat (9)	152
Arianna Storrs-Barbor	154
Joshua Burness-Smith (10)	155
Zoravar Udassi (11)	156
Robbie C (9)	157
Kamsi Iloka (11)	158

Ravenscote Junior School, Camberley

Anishka Sharma (10)	159

Rokeby School, Kingston Upon Thames

Ruben	160

Seadown School, Worthing

Surealia Smithson (11)	161
Faye Bowles (12)	162
China-Rose Smith (10)	163

St John's C Of E Primary School, Watford

Jacob Moon (9)	164
Ana-Rebecca Goncalves Geremias (10)	167
Sahasra Kesha (10)	168
Lekhana Yaralakattimath (10)	170
Roman Savtsin (9)	172

Tara Summer (9)	174
Tianyu Chen (9)	176
Rahela Bajenaru (9)	178
Indiana Bagga (10)	179
Evie Taylor (10)	180
Anisha Zain (11)	182
Coralie Turmaine (9)	184
Manan Kashyap (9)	185
Civadanya Sivasuthan (9)	186
Shivanshi Yadav (10)	187
Abigail Christopher (9)	188
Nancy Afua O' Sullivan (10)	189
Allegra Edy (8)	190
Frania Oledzka (10)	191
Amalia Rusu (10)	192
Prerana Prem (8)	193

St Joseph's Primary School, Stepps

Christie Blair (11)	194
Orla Rose (12)	195
Eva-Rose Brolly	196
Isla Lundie (12)	197
Cara Malcolm-Gourley	198
Hazel Izuagba	199
Aaron Connelly (11)	200
Liam Buckley	201
Aasiyah Raza	202
Lucy Hutchison (12)	203
Willow Miller (12)	204
Toby Agboola	205
Frankie Ferry	206
Megan Tang	207
Michael McKenna (12)	208

Swaffham CE Junior Academy, Swaffham

Nia Wood (11)	209
Evie Denman (11)	210
Arnie Ward (10)	212
Jessica Smith (10)	214
Neila Moura (10)	216

Jensen Frost (10)	218
Dougie Lawes (11)	220
Charlotte Chasney (10)	222
Lottie Cope (10)	223
Tommy Patrick (11)	224
Rosie Askew (10)	225
Gabriel Gomes (11)	226
Charlie Smith (10)	227
Aiden Nash-Choppen (10)	228
Oliver Starr (10)	229
Harry Todd (10)	230
Craig Russell (10)	231

The Kibworth Mead Academy, Kibworth Beauchamp

D Hanlon (12)	232

The Meadows Primary School, Lincoln

Primrose Worsdale-Mann (10)	235
Barry Winter (9)	236
Sienna Webber (10)	237
Cohen Tostevin (10)	238
Isaac Everson (10)	239
Jessica Cooper (10)	240
Isabelle Onyon (9)	241
Elisabeth Corson (10)	242
Joel Hirons (10)	243

The St Margaret's CE Primary School, Withern

Poppy A (10)	244
Camilla E (10)	246
Freddie Howell (9)	248
Sienna D (10)	249
Skye L (11)	250
Nixi H (9)	252
Skylar Greasley (9)	253
Alice W (8)	254
Zara L G (10)	255

Ursuline Preparatory School, Warley

Anaisha Rathi (8)	256
Jessica Spilkin (7)	258
Oliver Browne (8)	260
Ariana Wiggett (8)	261
Arabella George (8)	262
Katerina Stowe-Mici (8)	263
Ranveer Sandhu (7)	264

THE POEMS

Proud To Be A Cloud

I escalate to the furthest heights as I realise I am free,
I giggle from within, whilst I duck and dive,
Feeling full of glee.
I can see so clearly into the far beyond,
As I float through the mesmerising sky,
Smiling at my fellow clouds as they pass me by.
I admire the diversity of birds whilst they tickle me
As they fly.
Reaching further and further away from Earth,
Soaring so high.
I rest below the beautiful shimmering sun,
That illuminates the sky so blue.
Silently listening to everyone's dreams and wishes,
Hoping they'll come true...

Amy Abid (10)
Acres Hill Community Primary School, Sheffield

Pegasus And Me

Taking off, I soared so high,
Flying away on my Pegasus ride.
I flew to space like I was in a race,
Leaving behind me a stardust trace.
I looked down on Earth, it made me feel warm,
I remembered the meals I'd shared with everyone.
As I gazed into space, head filling with constellations,
I thought I'd just awoken my imagination.
As I flew into deeper space;
In the distance, I could see a rocket,
So tiny, it could fit into my pocket.
We flew for a bit through the stars,
They're so pretty, I wish I could put them in jars.
We flew through the dotted stars faster than Usain Bolt
When we saw giggling stars surrounding Mars.
As we were on Mars, Pegasus was neighing,
Whilst lying down, she was so funny, basically a clown.
As my feet were flat on Mars,
Aliens wearing name tags that said, 'Jack',
On them, came closer with sacks.
It was an ambush, surely,
I needed to rush out of there.

I jumped on Pegasus and flew far,
But one alien grasped on
And started to chew on my bag.
We fell back down on a different planet
That was as dark as night.
I looked around to see eerie eyes,
I nearly fled, but instead, I closed my own in fright.
And then I woke up, safe and alone in bed at night.

Lana Khawaja (10)
Acres Hill Community Primary School, Sheffield

The Best Game Ever

As I walk down the tunnel, I wait nervously to stop on the grass,
In my head, I picture my teammates shouting, "Pass!"
I'm waiting at the centre spot for the referee's coin to toss,
I look left, I look right, and get a nod from the boss.
I say, "Heads," and the referee's hand is tipping,
I look up and the shiny, silver coin is flipping.
It lands on heads and the whistle blows out loud,
And all I can hear is the roar of the crowd.
I cross the ball about forty minutes in,
From the stats, it's a game we should win.
It's half-time and the score is nil-nil,
I step off the pitch and my brain is just full.
With dreams of scoring the perfect one,
Or worst of all, I could just score none.
We step back out and the crowd are singing,
I have a feeling we might end up winning.
It's the eightieth minute and my teammate makes a run,
With a smile on my face, you can tell I'm having fun.
The cross comes in, a volley from a rainbow flick,
I run forward and try a bicycle kick.

The ball is soaring and it goes top bins,
Now, one more is added to our tally of wins.
We've won the match, what a game to play,
Top of the league, we're on our way.

Lucas Wright (10)
Acres Hill Community Primary School, Sheffield

What Should I Wear?

I can't decide what to wear in Dreamland.

I could wear red like the oak trees
That are scattered around in Dreamland.

Or should I wear orange like the seas
That have been ventured by vessels in Dreamland?

What if I wear yellow,
Like the blanket of grass in Dreamland?

Oooh, I know, I could wear green,
Like the everlasting sky dotted with glistening, minuscule stars and the gargantuan, radiant sun glowing in the corner of every civilian's eye in Dreamland.

What about blue like all the cars and paths that roam on the roads adjacent to the amber grasslands in Dreamland?

No, I've got the perfect colour.
It matches the towering buildings, the uncountable houses. If you haven't guessed: it's purple!
It's the perfect colour to wear in Dreamland.

White, it never lets you down.
At this point, you can even camouflage with how many white things there are.
The white wonders that spring up during summer,
Also, all the notes and coins are all white in Dreamland.

I think I know which colour I'm going to wear.
Gold, because I have got a gold jumper,
And it will help me because it is cold outside.
But, I can't forget that I was told to wear a jacket.

Aayan Sharma (11)
Adel Primary School, Adel

The Winning Goal

As I step out onto Elland Road's ground,
My dream so real, fantasy and reality are unbound.
With every stride, the crowd's roar swells,
As I chase the dream to score, with tales to tell.

As a left winger's fury, I heed the call,
To grace the pitch, to give my all.
I sprint upon the grass,
Intercept the ball through a thrilling pass.
The ball at my feet, I feel the surge,
As I dance and dodge with skills and urge.
Towards the goal, my eyes gleam bright,
Running through defenders, I aim for glory's height.

On the left wing where my dream takes flight,
I score the goal, it's the best ever night.
The crowd erupts in jubilant cheer,
I am the hero that Leeds United revere.

It's the ultimate dream,
Playing for Leeds United with my badge in full gleam.
I look up to the stand, my family so proud,
Scoring the winning goal, this dream feels like I'm standing on a cloud.

Jovan Lota (11)
Adel Primary School, Adel

The Diamond Monster

A diamond castle stands tall, high on a hill
All looks fine, but it hides a secret
Deep in the basement, there is a monster lurking
It has many eyes, all with night vision
Its body is made of diamond, hard as a rock
It hisses at those who see it
Yet no one knows what happens after that
For none live to tell the tale
Huge claws stick out of its feet, ready to slash
There is only one way to beat this monster
It is hidden in the castle's vast library
Its teeth are as sharp as knives
Able to cut through anything, like a knife on hot butter
To beat this monster, you will need courage
Take a bath in holy water
This will protect you from harm's way
Then, plunge a sword of diamonds into the beast's skull.

Diyor Aliev (10)
Adel Primary School, Adel

Is This A Dream Or My Imagination?

D istant deer sprint amongst the emerald grass which sparkles with the morning dew
R ain starts tip-tapping on my window; is this a dream or is this true?
E verything is still and quiet as I try to open my eyes, wiping away the morning sleep
A shout from downstairs startles me
M um is calling me down for my breakfast
L eaping up out of bed, I pull on my dressing gown; I can smell the bacon sizzling in the pan
"A m coming!" I call to Mum
N adia, my little sister, says, "The deer have been near this morning, running in the fields."
D id I dream this or did I see them from my bedroom window?

Nellie Gordon (10)
Adel Primary School, Adel

The Space World

Everyone here lives in space
There are infinite planets to explore
People build rocket ships to explore the endless void
They travel millions of miles an hour past the stars and planets

One particular person was on a very important mission
His mission was to find a planet that they could colonise on
And off he went to find the special planet
After a long time of travelling, he found a planet

The sky was blue and the clouds were white
The grass was green and the water was blue
The tree trunks were brown and the leaves were green
It was perfect! It had everything he could wish for!

He named it Earth.

Nayan Edwards (11)
Adel Primary School, Adel

Fear Of The Unknown

Sound asleep, body resting.
Pillow so soft, like a nesting.
Feet so warm, socks protecting.

Duvet wrapped, almost a cuddle.
Lavender scent, so subtle.
Sleep so fast, like a shuttle.

Sucked into the upside-down.
No other expression, aside a frown.
Falling, falling, down, down, down.

Anywhere is better; away, distant.
Soon passing out of sight; memory, existence.
Empty.

Hollows of darkness, depths of nothing.
Constantly on edge; running, running.
Fear of the unknown, although it's coming.

Drop!
Ground is near,
Too late, dread is here.

Liya Shahid (11)
Adel Primary School, Adel

Dreams Land

D ear land of imaginary dreams
R ed roses all over the land
E veryone there has an unlimited supply of chocolate
A t noon, you have to eat a chocolate bar or you fall into a
M assive pit of cotton candy and you have to eat it all
S mall, cute bunnies hopping beneath my feet

L ate at night, birds fly into your room and sing a steady beat
A fter that, they let you peacefully fall to sleep
N ow, sleeping soundly
D reamland is the place I would like to be.

Elise Mackay (10)
Adel Primary School, Adel

Wonderland

Wonderland, a wonderful place where dreams come true,
Evergreen trees and skies of florescent blue.
Magical, majestic structures stood in formation,
Unlike the real world, it's no abomination.
Pleasant residents reside in a mansion,
In this world, nothing is sanctioned.
Eternal dirt roads lead to love,
Beautiful heavens are miles above.
Bright blue oceans and golden sand,
An astounding rainbow bridge connects the land.
Wonderland is truly a jaw-dropping place,
It will always put a smile on your face.

Alex Vulcu (10)
Adel Primary School, Adel

The Scariest Dream In The World

S pooky, horrifying feeling travelled to my brain as I felt like something was behind me.
C reepy sounds came from the forest next to me
A feeling inside me told me to enter, so I did.
R ambling on a small path; a second later, a weird tree was in front of me. I wondered what it was.
Y elling came from the other side of the forest. I ran, then felt a tap on my shoulder. It was a monster. I was petrified. Then it jumped at me and I closed my eyes. Then, I woke up and realised it was a dream.

George Dickinson (11)
Adel Primary School, Adel

The Shark

I was swimming in my pool
And I heard a strange noise
So I went to check it out
I looked beneath my pool...
Only to see a shark!
I scrambled out of the water
And escaped just in time
I rushed up the stairs to grab some salt
And then I rushed back down
I chucked the salt in the water
Then the shark popped out
And came towards me
I tried to move back, but I was too late
It had already eaten half of my house
And now, it was about to eat my pet mouse!

Maryam Shah (11)
Adel Primary School, Adel

The Upside-Down

In the Upside-Down,
People walk with their hands on the ground!
The children go to school,
And the parents try to act cool!
They eat the bone instead of the lamb,
And bells don't go ding, they go bang!
You can see through walls but not windows,
And that is a problem when changing clothes!
Winter is hot and the summer is cold,
Old people are young and young people are old!
Despite the world being the wrong way round,
Everyone here is still sound!

Aris Padfield (11)
Adel Primary School, Adel

My Cats And I

My cats and I love to play,
We can't stop doing it all day,
When I stroke their fluffy fur,
They will give me a loud purr,
Sometimes they will catch a mouse,
Then they'll eat it in the house,
In the winter, they snuggle up tight,
But in the summer, they go out when it's light,
For a treat, I'll give them milk,
Then I'll let them sleep on silk,
We will live out the rest of our days,
Continuing in our own ways.

Noah Vigar (11)
Adel Primary School, Adel

Come To Dreamland

In Dreamland, there is cotton candy for clouds,
And thick, creamy chocolate for water.

In Dreamland, bushes are as wide as a football stadium and as tall as skyscrapers.

In Dreamland, there are trees made of pristine, crystal-clear blue gems and flowers are delicious strawberry lollipops.

In Dreamland, houses are made of gingerbread,
With red, creamy icing on top,
With multicoloured Skittles for lighting.

Nikolas Savic (11)
Adel Primary School, Adel

The Buffalo

Nails as sharp as knives,
Feet as large as bears,
There lived the buffalo.

With teeth as strong as an ox,
No animal would ever dare,
To touch the buffalo.

Don't let its furry skin fool you,
Because if you stroke it,
You will be dinner for the buffalo.

Even though,
The buffalo is strong,
It has the heart of a lion.

Gurnek Bhogal (11)
Adel Primary School, Adel

Sweet Dreams

My dreams are as sweet as a candy cane,
Full of sweetness and no pain.
Weaving down through a cola fall,
Dancing with gummy bears and all.
The everflowing chocolate fountains,
Next to the jelly mountains.
Never stop making me dream,
About all of these sweet dreams.

Naail Akbar (10)
Adel Primary School, Adel

Horror

D eath fell from the midnight sky
R apiers glistened in the atmosphere, piercing people's necks
E ndless blood streamed down from the clouds
A xes being dropped from the stars every second
M achetes rapidly swung at each other's ghosts.

Jordan Reid (10)
Adel Primary School, Adel

My Monster Is Different

My monster is different:
A chocolate lover,
A speedy runner,
A crowd stunner.

My monster is different:
A snow explorer,
A goalscorer,
A loud snorer.

My monster is different to all the rest,
But to me, my monster is the best!

Caitlin Smith (11)
Adel Primary School, Adel

What I Want To Be

A n athlete is what I want to be
T ennis, football and cricket, they play
H ockey, basketball and rugby too
L eisure is their life at home
E ating healthy food
T ricky sports, they play;
E asy, I find it.

Okan Dervish (10)
Adel Primary School, Adel

My Dream

D reamland is filled with happiness
R eal animals that are roaming around the land
E ndless fun that we enjoy
A chocolate river that you can hear from afar
M illions of sweets are scattered on the floor.

Leah Mackay (10)
Adel Primary School, Adel

Snow Is Falling

S now is falling everywhere
N early touching my nose!
O ops, I am trapped, but
W hy has the snow melted already?

Harpreet Virdee (10)
Adel Primary School, Adel

Lost In A Dream

I gallop, dashing away from the hospital,
Running through waterlogged ground - leaves falling,
I stagger, flat on my back; I see a blur, who is that...?
Unconscious, haemorrhaging, it looks like a Stone Age boy - that's strange.

I now know something is very wrong. The path I knew, where is it? It's vanished,
I bawl as loud as I can, no one answers; I search for help in my dad's bag,
No communication, actions work though; but he depends on me, what a friendship,
Honoured to have a friend for myself, I'm not sad anymore.

Solitary, wandering; we find a random cave, we hear a snivel,
Drip... Drip... Drip... A freezing, dingy, silent cave. I felt guilt,
Will I ever get out of this place, I haven't thought about this,
Snuggly teddy, Lily, bed, nice food, why did I do this?

Daisy Swales (9)
Bempton Primary School, Bempton

Lost In A Stone Age Time

I set off at speed into Mandel Forest,
No familiar sights - muddy, overgrown and shut off from the city,
Dropped! I saw a glimpse of a shiny thing,
Unconscious, blood making the sand flush, boy frozen in time.

Everything had vanished, overgrown, shut off -
I had travelled back in time,
I exclaimed, "Help!"
I felt a tear roll down my eye; no one replied,
I gave him the ancient spear and I trusted him,
I felt like I was surrounded by people I trusted.

Heading towards Deadman's Cave; suddenly, I heard squealing,
Splash, splash, splash! Scared, cold and alone,
I want to see my family, am I ever going to survive?
I want to get into my bed and snuggle my teddy.

Louis Robson (8)
Bempton Primary School, Bempton

The Forest

I sprinted away from my parents in hospital,
Tall green grass; leaves hanging off the branches of the spooky trees,
Crashing to the ground, a glimpse of a blur was seen,
Struggling to survive, a black-haired boy, barely breathing.

Paths had vanished, everything had changed,
I screamed for help as I searched through my dad's bag,
On this magical journey, grew a friendship so grand,
I was finally comforted by the boy I met.

Pushing through the vines, trying to find Mothga,
We heard that howling once again,
Silence, thunder booming, I felt like it was on me,
Will I ever get home?
Snuggle doggy, warm bed and my favourite food.

Elizabeth Hakner (8)
Bempton Primary School, Bempton

Stone Age

I bolted up the road into the dark,
I slipped down into the overgrown, damp, muddy forest,
I kept slipping, faster, I saw a blur in front of me,
Passed out, his cut head bleeding badly on the sand, the boy looked at me.

I was sure there was a path there, no sign of the hospital,
I searched in Dad's bag, looking for something to cover the blood up,
I took his hand, handing him the spear so he trusted me,
I was not alone, I felt safe and warm inside.

We went to Deadman's Cave to find his sister,
Silence, scary, mossy,
Will I ever get home?
Cuddly teddy, soft cats, seeing my family and playing with my toys again.

Ezri Wilson (7)
Bempton Primary School, Bempton

The Cave

I ran away from the hospital, away from my parents,
The muddy, dark forest where gloomy trees grew was all around me,
Crashing into a rock, I saw something in front of me,
Suffocating, blood flooding down the river, an injured boy.

A place unknown, with no sign of home, I stared around,
I searched for help in the bushes, but no one replied,
On this journey, we became friends for life,
I had someone to trust along this path.

We heard a cry which sounded like a baby's,
But it was a wolf cub's,
Horrifying, damp, mossy,
I really want to get out of here,
I want to snuggle with Dara at home.

Isabelle Butler (7)
Bempton Primary School, Bempton

Back In Time

I bolted down the road from the hospital,
Muddy ground and leafy trees, I ran through the forest,
Falling on the ground, a blur in my eye in front of where I am,
Collapsed, red blood pouring down the river, the boy froze.

The path I knew wasn't there, I had travelled back in time,
I screamed for help - nobody answered me,
I handed him a spear and he came, a friend for life smiling,
Somebody I trusted, he felt trustworthy and safe.

So strange, I heard a noise in the cave,
Gloomy, strange and quiet,
Am I ever going to get out of this forest and see my family?
My dad, snuggling my dogs, cosy bed.

Charlie Hickie (9)
Bempton Primary School, Bempton

Back In Time

I sped and ran down the road,
Sticky mud, leafy trees and spiky bushes,
Tripping over a rock, a person lay on the floor,
Breathing slowly, opening his eyes, Stone Age boy.

Time travelled, an unfamiliar place, nothing looked the same,
I looked in the forest for help - there was none,
Looking and smiling, we were happy, new friends,
Happy and excited, I had someone beside me -
Someone trustworthy.

We walked to the Deadman's Cave and heard whimpering,
Terrifying, scary, *drip*,
All I want is to see my family - will I ever get home?
Snuggling into my warm bed, having the best dream.

Harvey Lord (7)
Bempton Primary School, Bempton

Lost In A Fairy Tale

I raced down the hill, from the hospital to the forest,
Dark and gloomy, everything was so swampy,
Stumbling, I saw a shadow,
The shadow was dark and mysterious,
A boy was stood in front of me.

Frozen in time, everything was different,
Stone Age creatures all around,
We were now best companions; we smiled at each other, I gave him a spear,
My friend was reliable, I felt safe and protected.

We walked to the Deadman's Cave and all of a sudden, I heard a howl,
Silent, eerie, freezing,
I started to question myself: will I ever see my family again?
Warm hugs from my parents, I missed them.

Ines Braithwate (9)
Bempton Primary School, Bempton

The Cave

I bolted away from the hospital,
Dark, overgrown, scary trees,
I slipped over a rock, then I saw something unfamiliar,
Face down, blood flooding, a boy with a cut on his head.

Everything was different, everything looked unfamiliar to what I knew,
I yelled for attention - but no one replied,
Looking and smiling, we knew we could trust each other,
Finally, someone to trust, I was not alone.

Harby and I headed towards Deadman's Cave,
We heard something strange.
Pitch-black, soggy, damp,
Get me out of this place, let me go home,
A big hug from Mum, Dad, my brother and my sister.

Faris Watti (8)
Bempton Primary School, Bempton

The Cave

I ran and ran from the hospital,
Dark, muddy forest all around me,
Crash, there is something unfamiliar in front of me,
Unconscious, blood flooding the sand, a boy from the past.

The path had completely vanished and was replaced by leaves,
I looked in my backpack for help but no one answered back,
On this magical journey, smiling at our new friendship,
Someone I could trust, I wasn't alone.

Harby and me went to the cave's huge mouth,
Dark, scary, terrifying,
All I want is to get out of this dark, muddy cave,
See my dog, have a hot chocolate and sit next to the fire.

Maxi J (6)
Bempton Primary School, Bempton

Lost In The Cave

I leapt down the road, escaping the hospital,
My feet sunk in the mud of the forest, a tear rolled down my face,
Flipping over, a sudden blur in the corner of my eye,
Unconscious, blood gushing out, running down the river.
A Stone Age boy lost in time.

The path I had known had vanished in seconds!
Stone Age creatures all around,
Handing him the spear, friends forever,
Staring into his eyes, I felt safer than ever.

Wandering alone, we approached the cave -
A cry in fear!
Moist, wet, *drop*,
Will I ever appear again?
Snuggled up on the sofa, watching TV.

Josie Noble (9)
Bempton Primary School, Bempton

Back In Time

I bolted down the road, escaping the hospital,
Dark and creepy trees, they looked haunted,
Suddenly dropping down, something lay in the river...
Knocked out, barely moving; he was alive, he came from the past!

The whole place was unknown - I travelled back in time,
I searched in the wilderness for help in my dad's bag,
We travelled together, left, right and centre,
He trusted me, I trusted him, I wasn't alone.

We found a creepy cave and heard a squeak,
Alone, damp and mossy,
Will I ever see my parents and sister again?
Nice warm cover and a nice fluffy pillow.

Rory Hutson (8)
Bempton Primary School, Bempton

Stone Age

I sprinted out of the hospital - heart pounding,
Down into the forest, tall, ancient trees surrounded me,
I slipped and saw a weak blur,
Frozen in time, a Stone Age boy in the river, face down.

Suddenly, everything changed; a storm was coming,
I searched my backpack for anything to help,
In this puzzling world, we buried the hatchet,
I was slowly feeling warmer and warmer.

We were solitary, finding our way to the mouth of the cave,
Moist, unilluminated, *drip*, I heard the cave...
Will I ever go back home?
Going home, back to my routine, nice and warm again.

Albie Warrington (9)
Bempton Primary School, Bempton

Back In Time

I ran away from the hospital,
Brown, muddy mud and big trees,
I slipped on a rock, seeing a strange creature in the river,
A knocked-out boy was bleeding as the water turned red.

The path that I knew had disappeared, everything was different,
I shouted for help as loud as I could,
But no one responded, so I checked in my dad's bag,
I handed him the spear, friends for life,
I felt warm and safe with my friend.

I looked at Deadman's Cave, it looked strange,
Frightening, wet, cold,
All I want is to get out of here and just go home,
I want to see my cat.

Jack Collins (8)
Bempton Primary School, Bempton

Back In Time

I ran and ran, far from the hospital,
Slippery grass and tall trees,
Tripping on a rock, I saw a strange black shadow of something,
Face down, flooding the sand, a bleeding boy.

Unknown path, this place had changed,
I tried to get help but no one came,
He trusted me and I trusted him,
We travelled together, friends forever,
Warm and hopeful; all of a sudden, I was safe at last.

Alone, wandering, we heard something cry,
I think it might be Mothga,
Quiet, terrifying, alone,
How will I get back home?
Cosy teddy, home-made cookies, seeing my family.

Eden Patchett (8)
Bempton Primary School, Bempton

The Cave

I sped down from my parents into Mandal Forest,
Muddy rocks, hard, overgrown and dark,
Tumbling on a rock, seeing an unfamiliar object,
Unconscious, desperate to survive, a boy in trouble.

The ancient path just vanished, everything I knew had disappeared
I searched for help but all that replied was an echo,
We travelled so far, smiling, face to face,
I felt safer with someone who lived there.

We pushed vine after vine to the mouth of the cave,
Damp, quiet, alone,
In this mess, will I get home?
To my bed, snuggling my blanket.

Toby Hogg (8)
Bempton Primary School, Bempton

Stone Age

I ran away into the forest,
I slid in the dark, scary, wet, muddy forest,
Tripping over a rock, a person lay on the floor,
Breathing slowly, opening his eyes, a Stone Age boy,

Time travelled an unfamiliar path,
I looked in the forest for help, there was none,
Looking and smiling, we were happy together, a new friend,
Happy and excited, I had someone beside me,

We walked to Deadman's Cave and heard whimpering,
Scary, wet, damp,
All I want is Mummy - will I ever get home?
Dreaming of being home, cuddling Mummy.

Olivia Colman (8)
Bempton Primary School, Bempton

Stone Age

Escaping the hospital waiting room,
Slipping and sliding my way through the forest,
Trip, there is something in front of me,
Face down, frozen in time, an injured boy.

Frozen in time, everything was different,
Stone Age creatures all around,
Looking and smiling; we were happy together, a new friend,
Happy and excited, I had someone beside me.

We walked to Deadman's Cave, I heard crying,
Drip, damp, dark,
I want to go back to my family,
Cosy bed, warm house, snuggly dog.

Chester Barker (8)
Bempton Primary School, Bempton

Back In Time

I sprinted out of the hospital,
Towering, overgrown trees everywhere,
Trip, I saw a strange object near me,
Face down, not breathing, frozen in time, a small boy.

Different path, everything has changed,
I screamed for help but no one answered,
On this exciting journey, I made a new friendship so nice,
I felt safe with my new friend, away from the dangerous path.

Alone, walking with my friend, we saw something weird,
Wet, damp, dark,
Will I get out?
My beautiful family, my bedroom.

Jonathan Grouse (8)
Bempton Primary School, Bempton

My Mythical Snow Land

It is a snowy day in New York City,
The famous dancer was with her dance group.
The fairies were flying with the butterflies.
One of the fairies said, "Hi, wizard."
The wizard was excited to see the dancer.
The fairies got there first and were like:
"Do you want to come to our house?"
The dancer said, "Yes."
The fairies said, "Okay."
Their house had a butterfly door,
A mushroom roof and wooden windows,
It was light pink at the front of the house.
The dancer said, "I like it here,
The sunset is as pretty as a flower."
The dancer was like, "Do you have a mum?"
They said, "Yes, we do."

Maddie Vaughan (10)
Clements Primary Academy, Haverhill

The Portal In The Witch's Cottage

One dream ago,
I was walking in the woods,
When I saw a cottage.
I went in and sat on a chair,
That looked a bit broken.
I thought it felt weird,
Like there was a hole in the middle.
I checked it and...
There was a portal!
I put my hand in it to see if it was real...
Wow! Where am I?
I could see spiders and snakes with tails,
Cobwebs in corners that looked terribly disturbing.
I didn't know where I was.
Oh, look! The portal's back!
I went into the magical portal...
I was back in the cottage,
But it was all dark,
Like the lights had been turned off.
Arghhh!
W-w-what was that?

Leah Moore (10)
Clements Primary Academy, Haverhill

Fantasy Land

In this fantasy land, there is a terrible king
and a miserable queen.
Me and my friend stumbled into a huge hole,
And somehow ended up in a fantasy land.
I mean, it's a fantasy land; we love it here!
There are so many fairies and unicorns,
And the sky is bright pink and purple.
On the first day of being here,
We drank Pepsi out of a dripping pipe,
And ate candyfloss, but then we met the king.
He said, "What are you doing in my kingdom?"
We said sorry and he calmed down.
On our way out, we both saw a house,
A candyfloss house!

Pixie Probyn (9)
Clements Primary Academy, Haverhill

Sunset Birds

C olourful birds flying in the sky
O n the clouds, there's a chocolate house with sweets
L ive there and you'll have lots of treats
O ver the mountains, there's a swift and a sway
U nder the clouds, the children come out to play
R un and try to catch the birds
F alling with a bang and a crash... you won't get hurt!
U nder the clouds and over the mountains, the sunset birds dance in the sky
L ots of colourful birds flying in the sky; the lovely birds say goodbye!

Bonnie Lisher (9)
Clements Primary Academy, Haverhill

Wonderland And Deathland

Deathland is death, Wonderland is not,
So many sweets in Wonderland,
The roller coasters are as red as a rose.
I go to Death Land, so high in the sky,
Fire shoots from the clouds.
Why can't it rain sweets like in Wonderland,
Or just have better things?
All the swings are on fire, swinging so high,
Bang! A noise came from Wonderland.
Oh no! It is falling down so low.
Everyone cries and screams,
Someone sees it coming back up,
But it's not Wonderland,
It's another Deathland...

Maria Owczarek (10)
Clements Primary Academy, Haverhill

Life Is A Nightmare

L iving is scary sometimes
I am scared
F inding monsters
E ating bugs

I s my life
S pooky cobwebs

A nightmare

N ow, I was terrified
I was in an abandoned building
G lancing behind me
H itting the rocks
T his time, I saw a
M enacing man
A ll the way to the right
R unning as fast as I could; he started to give chase
E ldritch, he was Eldritch.

Isabelle Smith (10)
Clements Primary Academy, Haverhill

Wonderful Nature

Beautiful, lovely, colourful flower
Shining in the sunlight within the grass
Pretty petals; long, green stem up so high
The big, bright sun gazing down
At the long, swishy grass
Long, tall trees that are taller than me
The tiny, microscopic insects hunting their prey

The dark and bright shades of green leaves
The chattering of the children in school
The loud ding-dong of the church bells
The chirping sound of the birds above my head
Our surroundings are so magnificent.

Amberina Shahzad (10)
Clements Primary Academy, Haverhill

Dreamland

The clouds are as tasty as cotton candy,
The unicorns are as sparkly as stars,
The flowers are as tall as trees.
Butterflies gliding in the sky,
Sweets falling from the clouds,
Here come the unicorns - *Up! Up! We go!*
Poof! We transform into dazzling pink and purple dresses,
With shiny, gold heart belts in the pretty sunset,
Shiny crowns floating on our heads,
With diamonds all over,
We then drift back to Dreamland again.

Scarlett DeCruze (9)
Clements Primary Academy, Haverhill

The Dream

It's upside down in Dreamland.
The sky is as green as an emerald,
And the floor is as white as candyfloss.
Birds chirp at my feet,
The butterflies sway in the wind.
I see clouds beneath me,
Then they suddenly turn grey,
Then rain comes up.
I have to run; no time for fun.
And then I wake up in my bed.
"What happened?" I said.
"I guess it was all in my head,
I guess I'll go back to bed..."

Anaya White (10)
Clements Primary Academy, Haverhill

Lavender Dreamland

Lavender, lavender, where do you bloom?
In this field for me and you.

Lavender skies turn purple at night,
Sunset fills the western sky,
With huge butterflies fluttering around,
While crickets play their song,
As twilight fades into nightfall.

Petals of lavender come through,
As spring approaches.
Lavender sways through the cool breeze,
The grass is covered with lavender,
And a lot of ponies.

Ifra Saeed (9)
Clements Primary Academy, Haverhill

Dreamland

It snows every day in Dreamland,
It's cold and wet in Dreamland.
Snowflakes drop on my house,
Making everything snow white,
Glistening like the stars in the sky.
The children shout and jump about,
They build the snowman nice and high,
And more snow falls from the sky.
I see it all from my frosty window.
It snows every day in Dreamland,
It's nice and cosy inside my house,
In Dreamland.

Cian Jeffrey (9)
Clements Primary Academy, Haverhill

Dreamland

It snows every day in Dreamland,
Everyone plays with it,
But there's a place called Wonderland.

There are flying unicorns and pink grass,
Beautiful green cliffs,
And clouds that look like cotton candy,
With a beautiful, shimmering rainbow sky.

And trains full of clouds,
And buses made out of candy,
And houses made out of chocolate.

Ruvar Marume (9)
Clements Primary Academy, Haverhill

Space Dreams

The sky was as dark as a bat,
A dark house was in front of me.
Soon, it disappeared into the dark.
I saw a scary doll,
I ran as fast as lightning.
I reached the end of a new world,
It was still dark but I could see the stars.
I saw a rocket, so I got in it,
I started to fly to space.
I travelled to all the planets,
Suddenly, I woke up at home.

Stephanie Biko (10)
Clements Primary Academy, Haverhill

Dragon In Dreamland

The sky is pink in Dreamland,
Everything is peaceful until night.
The dragon is as purple as a plum.
The night sky is as dark as a cat.
Haunted houses are formed,
The houses are as blue as the sea,
And the tiles are as dark as night.
The dragon's wings sway gently in the air,
And the houses' plants dance in the cold night air.

Robin Lee (9)
Clements Primary Academy, Haverhill

My Mythical Home

My mythical house is amazing,
The clouds are like cotton candy,
The house is like a massive sweet palace,
The sky is as blue as a sour blueberry,
The door is made out of chocolate and sticky toffee,
When the sun finally sets,
It is as pretty as a pink blooming flower,
The house smells so good,
Like lollipops and bubblegum.

Talulah Kinsey (9)
Clements Primary Academy, Haverhill

Dreamland

Dreamland is a place where I eat sweets,
And I don't brush my teeth.
Right away in the morning,
I get up and look at my cotton candy grass.
Emeralds sparkling like the stars,
Creating a glowing pathway to my candy shed.
Hi, I've just had my lunch.
I had a lollipop and some emerald candy to eat.
Ta-da, da-da!

Jaxson Coker (9)
Clements Primary Academy, Haverhill

Dreamland

D reamland is a magical place where anything can happen
R oyalty and wizards
E veryone can come
A bright blue sky with white fluffy clouds
M ake anything happen
L ive on the moon or anywhere else
A nd get any job
N othing you can't do in
D reamland.

Diogo Santos (9)
Clements Primary Academy, Haverhill

Universe

Galaxies, planets, stars,
They float fast like cars.
Galaxies shine,
It's not really a crime.
Pretty purple planet,
All above the granite.
So many pretty things,
Hanging on with strings.
Glitter falling down,
As shiny as a majestic crown.
The stars are so bright,
They stand out at night.

Aisha Barros (9)
Clements Primary Academy, Haverhill

Football

F ootball all day long
O h, look at this stadium; it's so big and green
O h look, a goal!
T eams competing all day long
B ad luck, Messi
A h yes, Ronaldo is finally getting goals!
L ook, Manchester United won!
L ook at that trophy, so bright like a star.

Ariana Krasauskaite (9)
Clements Primary Academy, Haverhill

My Dreamland

The sky was so yummy,
It tasted like pizza for me and my friend,
And then it was snowing at the same time.
After pizza, we played in the snow.
My house was made out of candyfloss,
Cookies and sweets.
Here we are now - Up! Up! We go!
Poof! We had to return from the magic woods.

Ava Webb (9)
Clements Primary Academy, Haverhill

My Very Sugary House

Welcome to my dream house,
It has really good, sugary, sweet icing walls,
With a good, sugary candyfloss roof,
And a hard caramel door,
And I have lollipop trees,
And sweet cupcake windows.

Chase Hill (9)
Clements Primary Academy, Haverhill

It Rains Every Night In Dreamland

I wait for the sun to shine,
And for the snow to go bright,
As I see butterflies fly by.

The green grass shines,
In the bright sky,
And the rain drops in the night.

Patrick Cilheiro (9)
Clements Primary Academy, Haverhill

Untitled

Beautiful butterfly,
Flying so very high
It could almost touch
The wonderful sky.

Isabella Limpus (10)
Clements Primary Academy, Haverhill

My Future Farm Dream

Outside on the land, where there are only animals,
But don't forget the vehicles, machinery, and all the new arrivals.

More animals located behind the bales,
As the sky goes cold, the rain hails.
In the shed is an animal that produces milk,
With skin as soft as silk.

In my tractor, I like to rap a certain song,
I dream of listening to it all day long.
Running out of materials to keep the farm strong.
It's freezing outside... this must be wrong!

In winter, water flowed,
Whilst in summer, the fields were mowed.
Farming is stressful, more animals born in the dark,
Buried in the straw is a calf - not a shark!

As I dream big, my farm will be the best,
But first - my cows have to pass their TB test!

Jake Pugsley (11)
Egloskerry Primary School, Launceston

Can You Hear Me, Old Friend?

I'm full of sadness and despair, sitting on this wall.
While everyone is out celebrating the end of this big war.
I see air balloons flying up into the night sky,
While I'm sat here, wondering if I could've saved your life.

The poppy fields go on and on,
The distance goes so far along.
The shining stars are all lit,
Families at home sobbing over those who did not make it.

The cold, dry tears falling down my face,
Dreaming how they got to choose your fate.
Flashbacks haunt my dreams, memories coming back.
Replaying in my head that terrible attack.

Bullet shots getting louder and louder,
How will I ever last without you, my dear old friend?
Hundreds of graves before my eyes.
Will we ever meet again?

Invasion sights are coming back,
Blood, bullets, these are the memories I would love to lack.
So many lives have been lost,
The innocent soldiers paid the very difficult cost.

Digging trenches full of rats,
My head is dizzy like I've been hit with a bat.
Screaming, shouting, running around frantic,
Boats, submarines, all sailing over the Atlantic.

Wherever you are in heaven,
Maybe we will meet again,
My dear old friend.

Poppy Ranson (10)
Egloskerry Primary School, Launceston

Dream World

Once upon a dream,
There was a land of magic.
In a place called Dream World,
Nice, future nightmares and funny, of course.
I was too keen!

I walk around to see the seven lands,
But I see a massive black hole and...
It smells like a campfire with toasted marshmallows.
All of a sudden, I heard a faint, "Hello."

It was a worker,
But how could this be?
Was I in a dream or not?
I followed the guy like a stalker.

I asked where we were but he didn't respond,
I ran into a place called Devil's Dreams,
It was petrifying.
I saw a magic wand.

Dreams, dreams, dreams and dreams,
So many to visit, I found the black hole.
It's where all forgotten dreams go,
I heard glass shatter like a bowl.

I went to my future dreams and saw,
Me as an adult,
I looked old, wrinkly and mean.
Then, I went to the past and saw,
Me sleeping when I was a baby,
Having a good dream.

Aaliyah Mee (10)
Egloskerry Primary School, Launceston

Future Farm

My dream is my future,
I want it so bright,
I would love to be a vet,
Live on a farm,
And have a good rest of my life.

In the spring, we would start to calf,
Getting more and more, so we get the amazing gang.
Spread some silky straw and give them some corn,
Newborns are smooth like a baby's hand.

Mowing, bedding, baling in the summer,
Feed the animals with joy and wonder.
Don't forget it's the machinery that helps,
It would be too hard to do it ourselves.

After summer, it's a normal routine,
Milking the cows, feeding the ducks,
And checking we have eggs for tea!

Now, it's winter's turn,
We stop milking.
Feed cows silage,
And have a nice Christmas.

As quick as a flash,
More years go round like that,
I start to get older,
So my children start to help...
I hope this comes true!

Ellie Bloye (9)
Egloskerry Primary School, Launceston

Dream

Have you ever had a dream?
Were you in space, or on a football team?
Dreams are more than what meets the eye,
It's as complicated as Grandma's apple pie!

You've got dreams with rainbows and unicorns,
And others that have demons and sharp horns.
Ones with fields that end in darkness,
Ones with marshmallows that have no hardness!

Then you've got dreams for later in life,
Dreams when you have a house, kids and a wife.
Dreams for future jobs,
So you won't have to keep cooking on the hob!

Dreams of horror and nightmare,
Dreams of sunshine and spring.
Dreams of wealth and business,
After all, I really am going to miss this.

Max Uglow (11)
Egloskerry Primary School, Launceston

Level 0

A labyrinth of yellow walls,
A large amount of manor halls.
But how was I only sitting on a bench?
Hold on, what if it hears we are all missing?

Left to stand on the moist, wet carpet,
Seriously... this is scary. I forfeit!
I'm going crazy because of this buzzing.
Hold on... Who in the world is humming?

Suddenly, I am in an hour of horror,
When I hear a monster's roar.
Then I look up and say, "Who's there?"
Running to the sound, completely unaware.

I wonder what lies below,
A monster with a heart that's hollow.
As I run fast through the halls,
I see: 'Run for your life!' written on the wall.

Daniel Gunn (10)
Egloskerry Primary School, Launceston

Imaginary Friend

When life was young and time was beautiful,
She imagined me with antlers, like a deer.
She imagined me young, heart full of fun,
She imagined me to stop all her fears.

We played, we laughed; a box was a ship!
We never pretended guns.
Then, without warning, she started changing.
No more playing, no more parks, no more fun.

Then she moved house, worked in an office.
She forgot about me, her imaginary friend.
She took calls, worked late, and dressed very smart,
It seemed that playtime would end.

I wanted to leave, I needed to leave,
But then a baby cried.
My friend had a child,
I leaned over her cot and whispered... Hi.

Charlie Cox (11)
Egloskerry Primary School, Launceston

Demogorgon

Once upon a dream,
No people to be seen,
It was only my friend,
My friend was always mad.

I looked around the place in shock,
My friend was staring at me like a Demogorgon staring into my soul,
The thing I was confused about was him staring at me,
While lots of bees were following me.

Then I realised my friend didn't stare,
So then I found out he was a villain.
When I was in front of him, he shapeshifted into a demon,
Then I woke up and realised it was a dream.

I went back to sleep,
While the Demogorgon walked close to me.
A mystical dragon came out of a portal,
Just then, the Demogorgon got scared and ran away.

Harvey Blow (9)
Egloskerry Primary School, Launceston

Fairy Island

In a world where we can play again after tea,
People hear a lot of laughter, even me.
Children play all day,
But it's mostly in summertime, May.

Kids make paper planes,
There are lots of games,
Me and Jemma run,
We run a tonne.

Kids go swimming in the blue, beautiful sea.
Then we go and eat our tea.
I jump into the sea,
I am so cold because that's me

We jump on rides,
The roller coaster happily cries,
Next, the Ferris wheel,
It's a beautiful teal.

The beautiful blue flowers,
They are as tall as towers.
Blue, pink and yellow,
Maybe even a marshmallow.

Esmay Jackson (10)
Egloskerry Primary School, Launceston

The Demon Desert

I'm in a huge hot desert with nothing around,
Only the hot sandy ground.
But there is a dark tree with snow on it,
The only water is the snow,
That planes drop when they fly low.

I eat some of the snow,
But it takes me on a plane to another world,
Dark eyes follow me in the dark world,
Demons take me to a room with a screen,
But the door is locked and so I scream.

The screen turns off; the ceiling falls,
There is a button at the top of the room,
The button is as bright as the moon.
I try to reach it, but it's too high,
The ceiling falls faster when I see the door.

Emilia Powell (11)
Egloskerry Primary School, Launceston

The Black Void

A black void as dark as ink
Although if you could see it
It is definitely not pink,
Or any colourful or bright
Majestic colour.

Just imagine, a black void
With nobody to speak
And nobody to eat, that's
The black, empty void
The place I'm in.

It's empty, it's deep, it's dark, it's boring
I don't want to be here,
Help me!

All of a sudden,
The black void engulfed me
I started to scream.
I woke up in my bed.

It was all a dream.

Leo Lawrence (11)
Egloskerry Primary School, Launceston

The Mysterious Monsters

Once upon a dream,
I got trapped in a wonderful dream world,
A wonderful dream world... What am I saying?
A vast, deadly abandoned desert
With undreamable demons,
Lurking everywhere.

I started digging to hide,
But instead, I found gold,
The sight of the majestic iron hypnotised me
I've got to get out of here,
And get water.

The scorching heat started making me delusional,
I started seeing water,
But really, I was eating sand.
A boulder came rattling towards me,
Suddenly, four legs appeared...

Albie Barnard (10)
Egloskerry Primary School, Launceston

Clown

Once I had a nightmare, it was quite a scary dream.
Once I had a nightmare, one that would make you scream.
Once I had a nightmare, about a killer clown.
Once I had a nightmare, within a creepy town.

Once I had a nightmare, where I was in chains,
Once I had a nightmare, I don't even know their names.
Once I had a nightmare, I don't know what's happening next,
Once I had a nightmare, where I was perplexed.

"Help! Help!" I cried,
I think I almost died.
I woke up,
Except, did I...?

Amelie Cox (9)
Egloskerry Primary School, Launceston

Dreadful Dreams

Darkness, as thick as night,
Sometimes you feel like you are waiting for a fright.
If only you knew what was watching,
If only you knew what was lurking in the trees.

Mystical faces smother these woods,
Screams as loud as a banshee.
A city of trees dance in my head,
Like a million dreams in one.

Suddenly, I walk up with my head as big as night,
I ran to the stormy day outside where I met a pack of bears.
Now it has happened, the part I have been dreading the most.
I woke up with a zombie party host.

Sebastian Parsons (11)
Egloskerry Primary School, Launceston

Warm Summer's Day

Darting through the trees, quivering like a flame.
There is a hint of darkness on a warm summer's day.

Riding on my tractor, riding through the wind.
I'm riding on my tractor on a warm summer's day.

Everlasting light as I run along the stream.
Everlasting light as I walk through the grass
On a warm summer's day.

All life is here; everything is happy
On a warm summer's day.

My life is complete
On the everlasting warm summer's day.

Gregory Heywood (10)
Egloskerry Primary School, Launceston

Water World

Once upon a dream, where home is under water,
To fish, to whales, to coral of different colours.
Coral is home to lovely fish,
The whales are as big as a mansion.

In the rocks, lay a lobster,
With claws really big,
Sharks that swim around you.
No danger can be seen,
This is a world where dangerous animals are not mean.

The shark glides in the water,
Like a fish.
In the evening, the sun goes down,
Like it is underground.

Jack Cox (10)
Egloskerry Primary School, Launceston

Mystery World

Once upon a dream in a world full of lava,
And zombies with me and my dragon,
We were sent here to explore.
But in this world, there are no laws,
There is nothing worse than a world with no laws.
What a weird feeling, it feels really heavy,
I'm going to faint.
I didn't know this would happen,
It feels like a beast quest,
All just to fight the boss.
There's no point, let's just go back.
"Okay!" growls the dragon.

Jaydan Legg (9)
Egloskerry Primary School, Launceston

Stuck In The Backrooms

Touched down in a different dimension,
Dull carpets and patterned walls.
Buzzing lights filling my senses,
And a labyrinth of long walls.

Red flashing lights,
And lots of obstacles,
And signs that say:
'Run for your life'.

Standing still,
Travelling to a place with monsters staring,
They could attack, but they prefer not to,
Standing in a place called Level.
You cheated.

Jack Hawkins (10)
Egloskerry Primary School, Launceston

Nightmare World Awakes

As I fall asleep under the night,
I have a huge fright.
I have wings, so I think it's good,
But also I am hiding under my hood.

Darkness spreads, demons fly,
All of a sudden, I want to cry.
A tiny demon flies over my head,
And soon, I will be on my deathbed.

Fire roams free,
It's coming towards me.
I run for my life,
There is also a spirit chasing me with a knife!

Lola Gregory (10)
Egloskerry Primary School, Launceston

Seasonal Dream

In a magical world where dreams take flight,
Summer is day and winter is night.
Me and my friends have lots of fun,
While adults sit in the burning bright sun

I see the atmosphere full of snow,
While the wind really starts to blow.
Some people are shopping for Christmas candles,
While others are at home drinking hot chocolate,
holding the handles.

Chyanne Cathrae (10)
Egloskerry Primary School, Launceston

Once Upon A Dream

There was a person,
Who was stuck on an island,
With sheep and trees chasing him
And his hot chocolate!
He had to be up high in a tree
To get away from the sheep,
But then he realised
There was a shed bigger than the tree.
So he went into the shed,
He saw a nice blue Ford,
It started, and he ran away.

Daniel Humber (9)
Egloskerry Primary School, Launceston

Once Upon A Dream

In the world of Pokémon,
Charizard laughing over there.
Squirtle swimming in the white, blue sea,
Bulbasaur running next to me.
When you battle, they tell a joke.
Some hard as rock, some soft as cloth.

Liam Butt (11)
Egloskerry Primary School, Launceston

My Mother

My mother is the best, nothing like the rest
She looks after me day and night
She hopes my future is super bright
When I have a bad dream at night
She's the first to turn on the light
She gives me a hug and a kiss
Then she tells me it will be alright
She's caring and fun
And that's why I love my mum.

Ajwa-Noor Zeeshan (8)
Horton Grange Primary School, Bradford

In My Dream...

In my dream, spring is here.
Spring is here.
Spring is here.
Goodbye snow, flowers grow.

In my dream, spring is here.
Spring is here.
Spring is here.
Birds are flying, leaves are growing.

In my dream, spring is here.
Spring is here.
Spring is here.
Hello spring.
Hello spring.

Rosario Urbina (7)
Horton Grange Primary School, Bradford

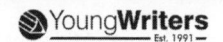

I Love Football

F orever running end to end
O nly dreaming of the win
O nce upon a time in a grassy field
T ackling players out of the way
B ooting a ball through the air
A gainst the wind with flair
L eaping up to score a goal
L oving memories made for all.

Muhammad-Musa Ali (7)
Horton Grange Primary School, Bradford

A Winter's Dream

Snowy magical sparkles dancing through the air
Glistening like the sun
Children screaming and having fun
Snow as soft as a blanket
Wrapped up warm
It really is fun
Winter has come.

Maariya Bismillah (7)
Horton Grange Primary School, Bradford

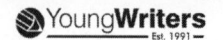

Clouds

What is fluffy?
What is white?
What can you see when the skies are bright?
What can float?
What brings rain?
What might be higher than a bird or a plane?
The clouds as I dream...

Anisa Ahmed (7)
Horton Grange Primary School, Bradford

The Beach

Do you ever dream of the beach?
Next to you, the sea,
Under the trees,
Watching the sunset,
Building sandcastles,
Hearing people's joy,
I love to dream of the beach.

Alyaan Amran (8)
Horton Grange Primary School, Bradford

Once Upon A Dream

I played football and I was happy
The coach was with me and taught me new tricks
I scored a winning goal
I won a trophy
One day, it won't just be a dream.

Emmanuel Adebambo (8)
Horton Grange Primary School, Bradford

At Night

The stars shine so bright
The moon is white
I only come out at night
I will give you a terrible fright
Don't worry though - I won't bite.

Minahil Noor (8)
Horton Grange Primary School, Bradford

Me And Daisy Save Christmas!

On Monday, me and my friend, Daisy, went to Lapland to see Santa,
Daisy said, "I am so happy that we are finally in Lapland together."
After Monday, we went to see everything there,
But there was no time to do everything, but I did go get a Fanta.
Luckily, Daisy enjoyed drinking Fanta, so we dashed over to the cafe like Prancer.

Tuesday, we went to go see Santa Claus in his grotto,
Then suddenly, he burst out with his famous motto,
"Ho! Ho! Ho! Hello to you both!"
An Elf arrived and whispered something to Santa,
"Sorry girls, emergency, I need to go to the workshop, pronto."
Me and Daisy decided to follow,
And uh-oh, we both fell into a hidden hole and bounced off a giant marshmallow!

We dumped, we jumped and we pumped our way off the marshmallow,
Only to find we were now in a tunnel, a hollow tunnel.
We ran in fear but also whilst having lots of fun,
We ended up at the end of the tunnel and we could not believe our eyes...

Santa was stuck under the presents, not a little amount, but a tonne.
Hip hip hooray! We saved the day; Christmas was here to stay!

Edie McDonnell (7)
Ireleth St Peter's CE Primary School, Ireleth

The Magic Wonders Of Christmas

In Lapland, me and my friend were eating chocolate chip cookies,
We heard an alarm from the magic Snow Fairy.
She said, "Santa has got lost,"
We knew this would be a day to remember!

At 9pm, me and my friend read The Magic Creatures of Lapland book.
We saw Jack Frost and the Little Snow Boys and the Snow Fairy
And the baddest of them all, the Snow Monster!
The Snow Monster had taken Santa,
But he had to deliver all the presents.

Some of the elves started to cry.
The Snow Monster was going to ruin Christmas,
Mrs Claus said, "You girls are going to save Christmas."
We were shocked and very happy,
We got to go into the forest to look for Santa.

There was a dark spooky cave,
We saw a glooming brightness in the cave and decided to follow it.

Me and my friend saw the Snow Monster with Santa,
We got him safely back to Mrs Claus in Lapland.

The Snow Monster said, "I didn't want to ruin Christmas,
I just wanted to have a friend; nobody wants to be my friend."
We found him a home and he was happy.

Daisy Chapples (7)
Ireleth St Peter's CE Primary School, Ireleth

The Dark Footy Night

One football match on a dark night,
There seemed to be a ginormous fright.
It was a dark-clothed clown,
No one noticed the dark shadow we found,
The clown jumped onto the green wet ground.
He tried to stop the game but it just wouldn't work.
He thought he better step up his game!
The dark clown got a cannon on top of the stadium
And shot himself onto the pitch.
He went to the ref; he wanted to look at the shiny ball
And blow the whistle, but he said:
"No way, why would I let you do that?"
The clown wandered off furiously,
But the ref didn't know that
The clown was the king of all the clowns.
The clown wanted to get a whistle
And pretend that it was full time
And he knew it was illegal
But that's what he found fun.
The ref was incredibly cross
Because the clown locked him up in football jail.
To get his revenge,
The king of the clowns sent his servants

To stop the game once and for all.
And no one knew that he could,
He was the mastermind of the clowns.

Lennox Read (8)
Ireleth St Peter's CE Primary School, Ireleth

Tiny Land

I went to sleep and what did I see?
I looked around and everyone was tiny, I was too.
It was scary at first,
But I knew my friends were there too.
We all got together and had a look.
I said to one of my friends,
"Edie, pinch me!" and she did.
But I did not wake up...
I tried and tried to wake up,
I knew I had to do something but it was all true!
We played in the water and the sand,
But we knew we needed to make a plan.
We wanted to play,
So we noticed it was not too bad after all!
We played and played but something was not right.
It was not just me that noticed, my friends did too.
Edie said, "Something is not right!"
Everyone was sad, it was a boring land.
We knew we needed to get out of Tiny Land somehow.
The people were as tiny as Polly Pockets,
I asked for help but no one knew what to do.
I squeezed my eyes shut and made a wish.
I woke up in my bed at home and I was safe again.

Alba Dalton (8)
Ireleth St Peter's CE Primary School, Ireleth

The Floating Football Pitch

Once upon a time, me and my friend, Lenny, went on a rocket,
We were just outside playing football when we heard the rocket!
We were hypnotised by the rocket, then we went to space.
We saw floating sharks and had a floating race.

We went to explore the football pitch,
There were gold players like Haaland and Rashford.
Then we played a match, I was so enthusiastic.
The match ended 4-4, but we went to penalties!

We won on penalties, 5-4, it was the best day of my life.
We asked if the football players wanted to come home with us.
They said, "Yes, of course we will. Do you want our signatures?"
"Yes please, I would love it, thank you, but I have a question.
Do you want to live with us?"
The footballers said, "We would love to if you could get us a bed!"
Lenny was shocked. He said, "Who is this?"

Oliver Cush (8)
Ireleth St Peter's CE Primary School, Ireleth

Islands

I live in space, it is pitch-black! It is as dark as a cave.
S irius is my friend who lives on Mars.
L iving in space is cool, but it is like a maze.
A stronauts are always around in space.
N ow in space, there are islands which have collided.
D own underneath the black dark, there is a dark void.
S uper duper happy is how you feel in space because you float.

I have a friend with a spacesuit which is as bright as the sun.
N ow someone has fallen into the void and is not coming b-b-back!

S pace is one of the most dangerous places of all.
P ut on your spacesuit and prepare for what is outside.
A stronaut Bill, he told me his name, is my friend in space.
C ome and join me in space, it is so much fun.
E veryone is happy now we have a new king of space.

Ellis Maiden (7)
Ireleth St Peter's CE Primary School, Ireleth

Fairies Dancing

F airies flying one by one, they are very magical.
A mazing sparkles drifting from the sky, so pretty.
I n the fairies' dancing space, they like to listen and play.
R ainbow disco ball above your head shining brightly.
I see the fairies dancing around, shining like diamonds.
E veryone dancing before my eyes.
S o many treats in fairyland!

D ancing fairies flying up and down.
A nd don't forget about the cheerful rainbow puppies.
N arrow paths only for fairies with flowers looking beautiful.
C old fairy drinks include; orange, pineapple and strawberry smoothies.
I nside one of the houses are beds made of flowers.
N o one can hurt the fairies because they have special powers.
G emstones scattered all around, why don't you try and find them?

Ayla Askew (7)
Ireleth St Peter's CE Primary School, Ireleth

The Safe Zone

In my million-pound house,
I had a safe filled with diamonds,
Emeralds, bedrock, see-through bricks,
Platinum, obsidian, tiger's eye,
Amethyst and gold.

It shined as bright as the sun.
My safe was as full as my tummy
After eight hot dogs and two burgers.
The titanium safe beeped as loudly
As the postman knocking at the door.

As I entered the code,
My fingers started to wiggle with nerves.
The safe door crept open,
The bright light from the jewels filled the room.
As the jewels fell, they clattered
As loudly as a monster truck's engine.

My dad found my underground basement,
He was trying to steal my valuable jewels.
I ran as fast as I could and slammed the door shut!
The thief had lost and I still had my expensive jewels.

Austin Taylor (7)
Ireleth St Peter's CE Primary School, Ireleth

The FA Cup Final!

It was the FA Cup final -
Manchester United vs Manchester City.
On Man United's team, there was:
van der Sar, Rooney, Scholes and Ronaldo.
On Man City's team, there was:
Trautmann, De Bruyne and Haaland.

Me, Ted, Oliver, Lenny, Leon and Ellis
Got together to watch the game.
Man United had the kick off,
Paul Scholes was rapid!
Ederson came out to stop him,
But Paul Scholes pushed the ball to the side
And skilled Ederson - It was 1-0.
Then Man City scored a goal, making it 1-1.
In the 32nd minute, Rooney scored a goal,
Making it 2-1.
The team talk at half-time had finished;
The game had started again.
Man United scored again,
van der Sar scored from a goal kick.
Making it 3-1, the game had finished
And Man United had won.

Austin Finnie (7)
Ireleth St Peter's CE Primary School, Ireleth

Animals

Once upon a time in Wonderland,
No animals were harmed or hurt,
It was a wonderful place to be.
It was a home of wonder,
One day, all the animals heard a scary noise.
They thought it was a human stomping their feet!
One of the animals was called Rosetta, she was a deer.
She was really, really brave,
She stood up to all of the animals
And noticed that the noise was a human.
She made best friends with the human,
She wasn't scary at all.
They wanted to be friends because the human loved
animals and the deer loved her.
The deer showed the human around Wonderland,
The human said her name was Lily.
Lily said that she wasn't actually a human,
But was, in fact, a fairy.
The fairy showed Rosetta around her house,
It was magical.

Florence Gardiner (7)
Ireleth St Peter's CE Primary School, Ireleth

The Sweetie Galaxy

In the galaxy, bright colours shine,
But have you seen the Sweetie Galaxy?
Probably not, with a lollipop moon and a candyfloss sun,
They are multicoloured and make you grin.

In the distance, I see a large house,
Made of chocolate and caramel tiles,
Buttons for the roof and a fountain of chocolate strawberries,
Yum, yum!

Also, in the distance, I see a 'For sale' sign on the house,
I think I'll need some candyfloss guards as companions,
I also realise I can eat them and make some more,
Even better!

I decide to buy the house,
Then my life changes,
Until I realise...
It's just a dream!

Willow Keel (8)
Ireleth St Peter's CE Primary School, Ireleth

Big Candy Land

My world is called Big Candy Land,
And I have a house made of sweeties and chocolate.
The trees are made of chocolate,
And the leaves are sweeties.
The grass is made of cookies
And the roof was made out of melted jelly.
This is our next-door neighbours' house.
Pixie Belle was walking across the road in Sweetie Chocolate Land and she saw her cousins.
She slept at their house in the cosy sweetie room.
There were sweeties and chocolates and a cosy bed.
In the morning, Pixie Belle and her cousins had a dance party.
There was chocolate and sweeties at the party.

Olivia Gaskell (6)
Ireleth St Peter's CE Primary School, Ireleth

Unicorns Are Beautiful!

Unicorns are beautiful with their
Sharp horns, unicorns fly over you
With sparkle and sprinkle dust
Over me, rainbow coloured with gleam.

Lovely and beautiful as can be,
Gleamy and gloomy, perfect as can be,
Unicorns have bushy tails,
As clean as can be.

Clicking hooves, brown and beautiful,
Pink hair as beautiful as can be,
Unicorns eat sweets,
Yummy as can be!

Sparkles in their hair,
Diamonds in their eyes,
They don't care what they want in their hair,
Unicorns are all beautiful in different ways!

Olivia Clark (8)
Ireleth St Peter's CE Primary School, Ireleth

Magic People And Dinosaurs

My magic teacher is beautiful,
Or some may call her a queen.
My house is made out of icy blocks!
It was dripping, slurping and banging,
When it was hot.

Then a T-rex came to eat some meat with me.
I said, "Hi," then I realised it was an old T-rex.
Then the old T-rex went back home.
A baby T-rex came to visit next,
Then I gave meat to him as well.

Then I said, "Bye-bye."
The baby T-rex went back home.
There was a huge bang,
As the snow fell and crunched,
It was so loud!

Nathan Roberts (8)
Ireleth St Peter's CE Primary School, Ireleth

Sweety Land...

Willy Wonka made lots of chocolate,
His home was made out of chocolate with a special fountain.
He went on his sweet way to get some moon sweeties,
It was so bright, he couldn't see.

Willy Wonka was trying every sweet to test it out,
Uh-oh! There were people floating about.
Within the chocolate sea,
The people tried to flee.

Willy Wonka helped them out,
By getting a large sweetie boat to pull them out.
One by one, the people were saved,
Thanks to Willy Wonka, who made the day!

William Galston (7)
Ireleth St Peter's CE Primary School, Ireleth

The Dinosaur And His Friends

The dinosaur and I are best friends forever.
I love helping the dinosaur.
He is extraordinary.
He is a helpful dinosaur.
He is my best friend.
He is not a horrible dinosaur; he is really kind.
He is amazing.
He is so nice.
Dinosaurs are an amazing species.
You are amazing.
You are really amazing.
Our friendship will never end.
Your roar is amazing.
I love you because you are my best friend.
Dinosaurs play with their friends.
You are so extraordinary.

Ted Archer (7)
Ireleth St Peter's CE Primary School, Ireleth

Chocolate World!

I am in a chocolate world,
I can eat all of the chocolate!
My favourite is the chocolate ice cream.

I spot my mum and dad.
They came here on a secret aeroplane,
I am so happy to see them!

The walls are made from chocolate bars,
The roof is made from white chocolate bars
And there are chocolate coins everywhere!

I use the money to buy chocolate strawberries
And munch them until there's nothing left!

Adam Colquhoun (7)
Ireleth St Peter's CE Primary School, Ireleth

Multicoloured Land

In my dream, there was a candy house
With a chocolate chip roof.
There was a caramel door, chocolate bar walls
And a lollipop chimney!
The cats and dogs were multicoloured
And so were the trees.

I decided to take a stroll down to the rainbow park.
The lilies and roses were multicoloured,
The people walking by had pink and purple hair.
Their clothes were green and orange and their shoes were red!

Elva Dalton (7)
Ireleth St Peter's CE Primary School, Ireleth

A Galaxy...

On the moon, I saw the stars,
A spaceman and a space dinosaur.
The galaxy is as bright as the sun
And the ground is as bouncy as a bouncy castle.

I played tig with my friends,
We bounced this way and that way, up and down.
We did backflips and handstands,
And played with the baby dinosaurs.

We had *super* fun in the best galaxy ever.
We can't wait to go again.

Parker Price (8)
Ireleth St Peter's CE Primary School, Ireleth

Outside

The bluebirds in the skies are as blue as the seas.
The green ground is as green as the leaves on the trees.
The leaves are as crispy as a French fry.

My door is made of chocolate,
And the roof is made of cotton candy!
The beach seas are so blue, it hurts my eyes,
And the rocks are so beautiful.
The birds sing loudly,
And the sun is as bright as sparkling jewels.

Elijah Knox (6)
Ireleth St Peter's CE Primary School, Ireleth

The Rainbow Dream In Candy Land

The rain in Candy Land was the colour of the rainbow.
"Wow, was that just a dream?"
It must have been because there was a monster too!
I was so scared because the monster was so big.
There were dinosaurs too,
Big ones and small ones, green ones and blue ones.
They matched the rainbow.
So maybe the dinosaurs liked Candy Land too.

Leon Bolton (8)
Ireleth St Peter's CE Primary School, Ireleth

The Beach

The temperature is very warm
And I have a pet snake called Sammy.
He protects me from the stripy, scary sharks!
He saves all the people from all of the sharks too.

Then all of the people were saved
And Sammy got older and older.
He was allowed to go outside
And slither to the beach.

Lachlan Roberts (8)
Ireleth St Peter's CE Primary School, Ireleth

Eat More Meat!

The T-rex said, "I must eat more meat."
He noticed a pile of meat,
He thought would be nice to eat.
Stomping and roaring so wildly,
His tummy started to rumble.
He ran so fast, he started to tumble,
Over, he fell, losing his dinner now,
The T-rex looked much thinner!

Zane Aboudi (7)
Ireleth St Peter's CE Primary School, Ireleth

The Dream Keeper

One night when I'm dreaming,
Away from all my scheming,
I fall into a magical land,
That is glamourous and grand,
Portals prance around me,
As if leaves in a tree,
Inside them, I see colours; pink, blue and gold,
Some are very faint, some are bright and bold,
I admire this curious creation,
Of my incredible imagination,
But suddenly, I'm interrupted,
By a shadow that's corrupted,
It's a big bloke,
And this is what he spoke:
"I am the dream keeper, in charge of everyone's thoughts,
I change perspectives in people's minds into what they ought,
I give good dreams and nightmares, depending on how I feel,
And no, this is not a dream, this is very, very real,
You're the only person that I have met,
So don't tell anyone about me or I will regret,

But for now, I am trapped in this dull, boring realm,
I have little, not even a fruit from an elm,
I want to be saved but I cannot,
Only if someone remembers."

Aasiyah Kolia (10)
Jameah Girls Academy, Leicester

Once Upon A Dream...

Once upon a dream, I had a peculiar night,
Where I met the Cheshire Cat and Tom and Jerry,
This dream was quite weird (not a lot, but very!).
I met the Ninja Turtles and a mean dog gang,
Then I heard a very loud *bang!*
It was Crookshanks from Harry Potter,
Using Hermione's wand.
"What on Earth is going on here?"
That particular bang was hard on my ears!
I had some gourmet cheese at a mouse cafe,
Where I even had to try a cheesy latte!
This dream was getting weirder.
What was I to do?
Just then I woke up and I thought, *phew!*

Amirah Osman (11)
Jameah Girls Academy, Leicester

My Imagination And Your Imagination

We have millions of thoughts,
Running through our heads,
But one of them is a dream.

Nothing fancy really,
It could even be a world filled with candy!
Maybe it's an adventure,
Or maybe you're soaring through the sky in space!
Maybe it's a sweet and happy dream,
Lying under the stars,
Or maybe it's your imagination.

Zaynab Pathan (11)
Jameah Girls Academy, Leicester

Space

When I go to bed,
I feel a glimmer in my head.
I listen to the wind,
Twirling, swishing around in the sky.
I wish I could spread my wings and fly...

Fly, fly through the dead of night,
Through the clouds,
Through the stars,
Through the hours of darkness.

I ride on the moon,
Listening to its serene tune.
Jump from planet to planet,
In the midnight sky.

I see the Northern Lights,
Green and blue, what a sight!
At the end of the night,
Just to hear the midnight clock chime,
I wish it could be night all the time.

And when my dream comes to an end,
And I realise that it's all pretend.

I'll be thankful for the moon, the stars,
And I'll be thankful that it's all ours.

Isabella Jaques (11)
John Locke Academy, Uxbridge

Night, Oh Night

You begin inside your bed,
A dream within your head.
At the time when stars unite,
When all light has taken flight.
Birds sing their final song,
With morning gone for so long.

Night, oh night, your twinkling star,
Its brightness seen by many afar.
The distant wonders of the moon,
Its beauty causing us to swoon.
Oh night, oh night.

Beasts come to battle,
As frayed nerves start to rattle,
Night, oh night.

A time when dreams overcome us,
When friends are among us.
A time for joy,
A time for rest,
A time to enjoy.
To expect the best.

Night, oh night, your twinkling star,
Its brightness seen by many afar.
The distant wonders of the moon,
Its beauty causing us to swoon.
Oh night, oh night.

When the time comes for night to be over,
Your thoughts will turn and cross over.
A crack of light splits the sky,
And all of your dreams are just a lie.
Night, oh night, I'll miss you so.
Does your time really have to go?

Caitlin l'Anson (10)
John Locke Academy, Uxbridge

Breaking Free

A nightmare is a dream that's not so sweet,
It's full of fear and things that make you retreat.
It's a place where your mind can't help but wonder,
And you're left with thoughts that make you ponder.

The darkness creeps in and takes over your mind,
And you're left with thoughts that are hard to unwind.
You try to escape, but it's hard to break free,
And you're left with thoughts that won't let you be.

But don't worry, my friend, for it's just a dream,
And things aren't always quite as they seem.
Just close your eyes and take a deep breath,
And soon you'll be free from this nightmare's death.

Remember that you're strong and you'll get through,
And soon you'll be back to feeling like new.
So don't let this nightmare get the best of you,
For you're stronger than you think, it's true.

I hope this poem helps you feel better,
And that your nightmares won't bother you in the future.

Judie Atoui (11)
John Locke Academy, Uxbridge

Foodie World

When I go to sleep at night,
I hop on a phoenix and take flight.
I fly far, far away,
Toward food that'll make you sway.
I fly toward the land of food,
Where I'm always in a good mood!

I eye goods in pure delight,
And gaze at the luxuries in sight!
Here, chocolate coins are currency
Whilst using, these kids squeal in glee!
You can blow a bubble in the air,
And use it to sail over this fair!
Many more things accompany this,
These all put folk in bliss!

Retreating, now I go,
Toward the sugar snow,
Slowly now, I glide away
It has come, a new day!
To this world, I bid adieu,
I go now, I have things to do!
Now, I'm asleep in my bed
With this story, I have read.

Anaaya Kale (11)
John Locke Academy, Uxbridge

Devil's Wish

I lay here tonight in my bed,
Thinking of all these scary things inside my head.
Suddenly, I find myself in this world,
I am scared, I feel fear,
Slowly, I feel a tear.
The floorboards are creaking: I am weeping.
The wind's whistle makes my bones feel brittle.
My hands on my head, I'm chucked into a shed.
Shadows loom, is this my doom?
A creepy clown.
Its malicious red smile laughs and chuckles,
It cracks a knuckle.
Blood on the walls,
Skeletons rotting in the halls.
My heart is drumming out of my chest,
I don't know how much time I have left.
I hear the clocks ticking,
My ears are ringing.
Dogs are whining, dogs are dead,
All I can see is their flesh.
Snakes slither up my arm.
I need to try and make myself calm
However, I can't, it's too much to handle,

The only light here is a small candle.
I try to find my way out,
I try to escape but there is no hope,
I guess I will rot in this place.

Tanaya Patel (10)
John Locke Academy, Uxbridge

My Dream

The trees and the breeze settle on foreign seas,
It's like a dream, what does it mean?

A mountain with snow,
Hunters that are the foe,
Lions and tigers in jungles so
Birds with great wings go to faraway lands,
Crabs and starfish nestle in sands,
It's like a dream, what does it mean?

The trees and the breeze settle on foreign seas,
Flowers that grow,
Plants that we sow,
Black and yellow buzzing bees,
And a butterfly jubilee!
It's like a dream, what does it mean?

I feel like I'm flying across the horizon,
My eyes burning as the sun brightens,
I've flown down - the grass as my resting place,
I look around and embrace,
It is a dream but what does it mean?

Ahana Madhok (10)
John Locke Academy, Uxbridge

My Nightmare

In the depths of darkness, fear comes alive,
Within these walls where nightmares strive,
A haunting nightmare.
As my heart pounds, caught in this eternal fright.
Animatronic terrors lurking in the shadows,
Each step I take, uncertainty follows.
But I muster the courage, desperate to survive,
Through this chilling bedroom where I strive.
With every passing hour, fear deepens its hold,
These mechanical beasts, their secrets unfold.
Jump scares and screams echo in my ears,
I'm trapped in this nightmare, fueling my fears.
But I press on, determined to prevail,
In this twisted nightmare where horrors assail.
A dread-filled domain, but to no avail,
I wake up and start dreaming again.

Vatsal Agarwal (10)
John Locke Academy, Uxbridge

A Glimmer In The Darkness

I go to bed and sleep
I count 100 sheep
The moon shines brightly upon my land
And fairies sing in the light, hand in hand
What a lovely day for me
As the bluebells flourish beautifully in glee

I jump on red and white mushrooms
Drink from the chocolate water in the washrooms
The twinkling stars sing their peaceful lullaby
While tawny owls hoot in the midnight sky
Red roses dance gracefully
The cricket band plays music filled with radiancy

But when morning comes, you have to go
I'll miss you night, oh so
But when you do arrive
I'll sing, dance and thrive
I'll miss you night, oh so, oh so
But when morning comes, you have to go.

Asya Javadzadeh (10)
John Locke Academy, Uxbridge

Another World

I think of another world in my head,
As I lay down on my bed.
There are various things there,
Like the bear that broke the chair.
And the mice,
Who always like to swim in rice.
Far away from the mice is a cat,
Who tries to eat the chubby rat.
And in the lake, there are some fish,
Who grant you a powerful wish.
But no - this is not the end,
There is an animal that always defends,
All of its wonderful friends.
However, it's got a lot of power,
And it lives in the tower.
It is none other than the deadly snake,
Who is always awake.
And even though the snake is very lazy,
No other world could be this crazy.

Amelia Kopczak-West (11)
John Locke Academy, Uxbridge

My Magnificent Dog

My dog is amazing
My dog is a beauty
He is the only dog ever loved by me

He is the king of my dreams
He is utterly supreme
His soft fur
His energetic heart
He stinks me out when he decides to fart
My life is lucky to have him as a part

Barnaby,
You are loved by me
You're amazing, you see
Chasing squirrels up the tree
Trying to get biscuits off of me

He is the sheepdog of pigeons
For scaring them is something he will always love
Jumping up to play with me
Sad eyes to say please
He is amazing, can't you see?
Goodbye! That is enough of me!

Leo Curtin (10)
John Locke Academy, Uxbridge

Life In A Bad Future

Smoke-filled air
Life is no longer fair
The society
Made to scare.

Life no longer thrived
Nothing had been revived
How can people live
In such a torn-down place?

Rubbish loaded the streets
The whole city was just downbeat
Rain relentlessly poured down
Which gave everyone a frown

There's no point trying to fight
In a place that has no light
What is hope
In a place that has people set to cope?

Help or not, it doesn't matter
People's dreams would only flatter
The sky was as blank as grey
Every individual day.

Daniel Harding (11)
John Locke Academy, Uxbridge

Flying

What a glorious feeling to fly,
With the birds up in the sky,
You can see planets like Venus and Mars,
Look further and you'll see the stars,
Spaceships, rockets and more,
Here, there is nothing to ignore,
I am flapping my wings in glee,
Who would like to leave?
I swoop downwards fast,
I see my friends, family and Pokémon cards,
I start to feel energetic,
I open my eyes with a click,
I see my pyjamas while waking up,
It was all just a dream that got me hyped up.

Adam Zarouk (11)
John Locke Academy, Uxbridge

Hope

Smoke fills the air
All around is despair
With nothing left to spare
No one's there to care
In what was once a place
Where people would share
Nothing is fair
Wait! What's that over there?
A glimmer of hope that can't be compared
Suddenly, it declared me out of this place
Now I'm back, prepared for my bed.

Ali Khan
John Locke Academy, Uxbridge

Unicorns

Do unicorns exist?
Do unicorns have wings?
Are unicorns the prisoners of prehistoric kings?

Are unicorns good,
Or are unicorns bad?
Are unicorns evil or maybe even sad?

So what's the truth about unicorns?
Can they magic little bows?
Are they just dreams or maybe nightmares?
I think we'll never know.

Olivia Arlauskaite (10)
John Locke Academy, Uxbridge

Realisation

My life has been
Unfortunate for too long.
Things are going completely wrong.

I lay in my bed with closed eyes,
I wait for the dread to dry.

I lay asleep in a dream
But I see a shining gleam.
Oh look, a million stars,
I have never ever reached this far.

Joanna Buaron (11)
John Locke Academy, Uxbridge

Dare To Dream

Dare to dream,
Dreams can be big or small,
Yet you can never have them all.

Dare to dream,
Hand in hand,
With no reprimand.

Dare to dream,
Like a dove with fleeting wings,
Your dream sings.

Dare to dream.

Varnika Badarla (11)
John Locke Academy, Uxbridge

One School Dream

I had a dream that school was shut
No English, no maths, no history, but,
Oh no, it's not a dream come true -
The virtual classroom is here to pursue.
The unlucky learners of JLA have come
Back to learning for just one day.

Sebastian Feneck (10)
John Locke Academy, Uxbridge

Football Mayhem

In my dreams, I arrived at a football match,
My curiosity pushing aside my fear.

The scouts were watching with excessively big doubts,
The coaches were there to implement their strategies.

The whistle blew and the game started,
The crowds were roaring, they needed help,
But not from the Pope because he was dope.

The players from the other team were defending,
While I pushed forward with the ball,
I passed swiftly to my teammate, but they got fouled.

The clock was ticking,
It was the last minute of the game,
Then the referee went to VAR,
And declared it was a red card
To the other player in the penalty box.

I wanted to strike the ball into the net,
Like Cristiano Ronaldo in a bizarre but beautiful way,
That would impress the scouts.

When I was getting ready,
I ran up to the ball and outside curled it,

With my left foot into the goal... *Bang!*
The goal shook violently.

The crowd roared with excitement,
The stadium shook as if it was going to collapse.
It felt like I had caused an earthquake.

I awoke from my dream to the sound of a phone call.
I heard my mum scream, "You have been scouted!"

Naik Kalkat (9)
Lyndhurst School, Camberley

The Flying Ship

I awaken to a fish with colours bright,
Is this an ordinary night?
It takes my hand and lifts me from the land.
Coming is a ship, still in the fish's grip.
It lowers and encloses me in its grasp,
I let out a gasp.
When I step in, the ship begins to spin.
In the sky, we begin to fly.
Hovering over rooftops,
I see the freshly laid crops of local farms.
It seems serene as we plunge into the marine.
A coral reef is in sight,
Again, we take flight.
On my way home,
It opens the dome.
I have arrived safely,
I see my cat, Baylee.
I hop into bed,
I hope Baylee's been fed.

Arianna Storrs-Barbor
Lyndhurst School, Camberley

Space Sloths

Space sloths, space sloths.
They climb trees,
They sail seas.

Space sloths, space sloths.
Their hair blows in the breeze,
And their favourite food is peas.

Space sloths, space sloths.
They travel the skies,
They eat a lot of pies.

Space sloths, space sloths.
A storm trampled the town,
And the space sloths came down.

Space sloths! Space sloths! Space sloths!

Joshua Burness-Smith (10)
Lyndhurst School, Camberley

The Great Fall

I fall through the sky,
Thinking of my favourite dish - apple pie.
I know this is my last blunder,
There is a bolt of lightning and a roll of thunder.
Hear my cry!
I look left, I look right,
What a sight!
Thunder clouds here,
Thunder clouds there.
No longer,
Am I in despair?
And then I wonder,
Why was he chasing me,
The hunter?

Zoravar Udassi (11)
Lyndhurst School, Camberley

Once Upon A Dream

Dreaming is like magic
You can be anywhere
Up, down, all around
If you can think it, you'll be there!

You can defy the laws of gravity
Make a land of your own
You can be as tiny as an ant
Or make yourself grow

The chime of a clock
Can break dream world apart,
Your true eyes will open,
And then your day will start.

Robbie C (9)
Lyndhurst School, Camberley

Meeting Sonic

I woke up and found myself nowhere.
A sign said: 'Green Hill'.
Then I saw somebody fast in the distance,
They gave me a scare!
It was Sonic the Hedgehog!
He was even faster than a hare!
Then I saw an eggnog,
Sonic's greatest enemy!
Sonic decided to beat Eggman up.
Then I woke up,
In my bed.
It was a good dream!

Kamsi Iloka (11)
Lyndhurst School, Camberley

January

Opening the window,
To a crisp blanket of white,
Making resolutions,
As our hopes and dreams take flight.

Anishka Sharma (10)
Ravenscote Junior School, Camberley

Upside Down Land

In Upside Down Land,
A dreamy world unfolds, so wonderfully grand.
Up is down, and down is high,
Imaginary creatures, oh my, oh my!

Giraffes with tails that reach the sky,
Candyfloss clouds with a mischievous twinkle in their eye.
Fish dance like frogs on a log,
Dreams flutter like a polka-dotted frog.

Loud laughter, a bubbly cheer,
As elephants giggle upside down, my dear.
In this topsy-turvy dream so wild,
Monkeys hoot like a mischievous child.

The sun sets in the east, rises in the west,
A dreamy notion putting sleep to the test.
Imagery paints a sky of lavender hue,
Where kangaroos jump with a backward view.

So close your eyes, let your dreams take flight,
In Upside Down Land where day is night.
A fantastical place where giggles expand,
In the magical dream of a 10-year-old's land.

Ruben
Rokeby School, Kingston Upon Thames

The Rock Band

Once upon a dream in a faraway land
That was filled with sand,
And a little rock band
With a tanned little bag.

In the rock band was a tanned little girl,
Her name was Pearl,
And she swirled and twirled.

When she was playing music in the band,
She fell into the sand,
And hurt her hand on the land.

She couldn't play the guitar,
Because of her scar.
Now she was sad because she couldn't be the star.

Then when she realised her scar
Was the shape of a star
She went to space and became a star!

Surealia Smithson (11)
Seadown School, Worthing

School

S afe at first
C an't understand why they left me alone
H alf an hour after lunch, I'm still alone out here
O nly a dream ago, I was laughing with the girl I can't find
O ff balance, trying to find my way back, thinking about last time
L ast time was different; different students and a different teacher, but it's the same school. Why did they leave me alone?

Faye Bowles (12)
Seadown School, Worthing

The Meadow

G reen lush grass under your feet
R are herd of horses far away in a field
A soft breeze hits you
S o lovely as you roughly touch the grass
S oft, you're lost in the meadow.

China-Rose Smith (10)
Seadown School, Worthing

Planet Eros

Once upon a dream,
Not a weird one, it seems,
I fly,
Up in the sky,
And through space,
To a place,
Called Eros.
A moon of Venus,
I land,
Have not planned,
What to do,
Until I hear a neigh,
I see two pegasi playing,
"Can I play?" I say.
Along comes a pegasus with a jewel on its head.
"This is the king of Pegasi," a voice said.
"Who are you?" I ask.
"I am Echo, the nymph queen of planet Eros,
I will show you around,
Although it is out of bounds
To let a human enter Planet Eros.
But you are a special one,

So come on, let's have some fun."
"You can ride Cupid," says King Pegasus.

"This is the temple of Aphrodite,
See how it gleams inside
With pride."

"This is Echo's cave,
Where she wore off without a trace,
But with only her voice left,
She felt betrayed."

"This is the river of Poseidon,
King of the seas,
He loves horses,
Even more than me."

"It's almost the end of our tour
Come to my castle, I implore.
This is where I live,
I love it here and never want to leave,
This is a magical place
For any race,
Of pegasi or nymph."

"Now, it's the end,
Please, come again

And spend time with me and more nymphs
And more of your pegasi friends."

Off I go, back into space
And up high, I soar into the sky
Back to my mind, I wake up

It was all a dream, it seems.

So, dreams are good,
Dreams are amazing for you.
Dreams are incredible,
And one day, they might come true.

Jacob Moon (9)
St John's C Of E Primary School, Watford

The Night I Never Woke Up

T he night I never woke up,
H enry bought his pup,
E veryone saw it.

"**N** ice day, isn't it?" said Mr Duncan.
"**I** t isn't so good. I still need to commit," I say.
"**G** rrrr!" growls his dog.
H e'd just had a jog.
T he dog bit and they both fell asleep.

"**I** p, ip, ip, ip," said the weird creatures.

"**N** ip, nip, nip," said the other weird creatures.
"**E** ip, eip, eip, eip."
"**V** ip, vip, vip."
"**E** rm, Duncan? Are you here?"
"**R** ip, ip, ip."

"**W** here am I?"
"**O** kay! Calm. I am lost and can't get out."
"**K** ip, kip, kip."
"**E** ip, eip, eip."

"**U** eap, ueap, ueap."
"**P** op, pop."

Ana-Rebecca Goncalves Geremias (10)
St John's C Of E Primary School, Watford

A Monster Daydream

I look up to see something,
On its finger, there's a ring,
Its face is like a circle - it's so round,
And it's standing fearlessly on the ground.

Yellow prickles all over its back,
Its mouth smelly, its tongue black,
One step at a time, it comes near,
And that starts bringing up my fear!

On its nose, there's a big red spot,
And its teeth look like they're going to rot,
Its fingertips are terribly long,
And when it walks, it makes a big dong.

Its ears are like the tip of a knife,
And now it's coming, I have got to save my life,
Its neck is craned, its knees are sore,
And when it sees me, it gives a big roar.

Its toenails are long, they're really sharp,
And it sounds the opposite of a beautiful harp,
It has one eye and it looks fierce,
And its eyeball looks like the sun in the universe.

I can see it now, it's in front of me,
I have got to move now, I want to flee,
It again gives a growling roar but I try to stay calm,
Suddenly I felt a hand on mine, like a soothing balm.

I shake my head and look around with dread,
I'm bent over my comprehension instead,
I look up and say with a gleam,
"What a scary daydream!"

Sahasra Kesha (10)
St John's C Of E Primary School, Watford

Secrets Of Dawn

Once upon a dream, under moonlit branches,
Where the starlight dips and the fireflies blink,
Journeys transpired, not overly sweet,
But microscopic barefoot feet, full of whispers, of wonder.

Through meadows full of unravelling secrets, where the mist trails like silk,
Charming knights ascend above milk mountains.
To cloud fortresses featuring towering, picturesque hummingbirds,
Dreams that become feathered and respond to the call.

Through stardust rivers with invisible waves,
They sail paper boats on a calm moonlit night.
Beyond desire islands where tales are spoken in whispers by the night,
And laughter takes control of you like an eagle.

For in dreams beyond legends, where wonder takes hold,
Little hearts grow wings of stories untold.
So, snuggle in close, let the moon be your guide,
Once upon a dream, adventures reside.

With murmurs of magic and starlight's embrace,
Dream of endless journeys in this wondrous space.
For courage and kindness paint skies ever bright,
Once upon a dream, let your spirit take flight.

Let the breeze away for a clearer future,
Through the moonlit sky,
The glistening sky beaming like a beacon,
For courage and kindness paint skies ever bright.

Lekhana Yaralakattimath (10)
St John's C Of E Primary School, Watford

Dream

As I'm drifting off to sleep,
I am stepping further into the deep,
Deep space, into the unknown,
Full of stars, planets and asteroids that glow.

I'm floating past so many planets,
Then I turn around and see my rabbit.
My best friend and me, here in a spaceman jacket,
Joining together for an adventure without a racket.

Let's explore the planet, Neptune; it is the furthest from the sun,
So we start to moonwalk and then we run.

Out of nowhere, jumps out a creature,
An ice blue alien with different features,
"Can I help you?" he says politely,
In the distance, the Neptune moon shines brightly.

All is aglow, illuminating with light,
Brilliant and beautiful, the sky at night.

I say to my rabbit, "I wish I could stay."
"We must return to your bedroom," my rabbit says,
"It will be breakfast time very soon,
We will be missed if we stay with the moon."

Then I open my eyes as the sun gleams,
I remember they were just wonderful dreams.

Roman Savtsin (9)
St John's C Of E Primary School, Watford

Me And My Spider (Who No One Knows About Yet)

I'm just a little girl dreaming,
But my dearest friend is not from a dream,
She's real enough, isn't she?
So when I have time to ponder...

I sit close beside my gloomy little spider,
All she does is spin, and spin some more,
She loves to spin her web all day,
But finally, at night, she decides to play.

Her web looks like my dress,
Which confuses us with eight legs or less,
My spider may not be a human being,
But a spider is my best of friends,
Who says a girl's soulmate is always a human?

Sometimes when my spider isn't there,
I sit and write in my book of different places
Where a child is crying and the sun is shining,
Both of which will not last,
For I am just a girl writing in my book.
The ink I use will stain all over the pages,

Like people's love, letters will wither away
And be left unremembered.
Things never last.
They break.

Tara Summer (9)
St John's C Of E Primary School, Watford

The Pirate's Dragon

A pirate with superpowers,
Sailed the seas with his crew,
In search of a treasure trove,
And a dragon or two.

He had a sixth sense,
Could see through the dark,
And when he was in danger,
He could summon a shark.

With his trusty sword,
And his powers so grand,
He battled the dragon,
And saved his merry band.

The treasure was found,
And the pirates were rich,
But the dragon's breath,
Was a powerful glitch.

The pirate used his powers,
To put out the flames,
And the dragon now tamed,
Was no longer the same.

The pirate and dragon,
Became friends for life,
And the pirate's powers,
Were no longer a strife.

So if you're ever at sea,
And you see a dragon fly,
Just remember this tale,
And don't be too shy to say hi.

Tianyu Chen (9)
St John's C Of E Primary School, Watford

Candy World

Even though I am so high in the sky,
The whole world is so colourful, I don't want to say bye.

When my unicorn lands, I fall on a bright pink lollipop,
So I stand and look around and notice a clock shaped like a shop.

I stand proud and think to myself, *where am I?*
After that, a chocolate bar appears and is called Skye.

I wonder if this is a secret, magical place,
Then all the other sweets came and started to race.

So I cried out, "Can I join too?"
They replied, "Yes, we'll give you a clue!"

We all had fun playing the game,
Then I told them the clues were the same.

One of the chocolates came to me and declared,
"We want you to be the Queen of Candy!"

I said, "Yes..."
But then I woke and wished it was real!

Rahela Bajenaru (9)
St John's C Of E Primary School, Watford

The Tiger's Life

In the forest every night,
A tiger roars, giving fright,
Who would dare to hunt such beauty?
Who would dare to hunt such might?

Running and pouncing with speedy feet,
With which we could never compete,
All we do is hunt and poach,
While they would never us approach.

What we need to do is act,
Together, we'll create a big impact,
Why should they deserve to die?
We really, really need to try.

Look at those stripes, look at those paws,
So worthy of life and our applause,
Creeping through trees, so very alive,
Killing to live, only to survive.

In the forest, in the night,
A tiger stands big and bright,
We don't have the right to hunt,
We're just trying to stand in front!

Indiana Bagga (10)
St John's C Of E Primary School, Watford

A Winter Dream

A winter dream,
As I lay by in the frozen snow,
It bites me cold and fast,
The cold rushes through my body,
Frosty and sharp,
Freezing my fingers.

A winter dream,
I've woken up in the frozen snow,
I don't know where I am,
Is this a winter dream?
As I stand, I can't feel my fingers
I can't feel my toes.

A winter dream,
I've walked for what feels like hours,
But as I walk, I think,
I realise that winter is not all bad.

A winter dream,
Winter is not all bad,
It is always beautiful,
In a strange, cold way

As frost strikes
The sky turns into a dark misty fog

A winter dream,
As the day comes to an end,
The blossom slowly comes
As we enter into spring.

Evie Taylor (10)
St John's C Of E Primary School, Watford

In My Box Of Dreams

In my box of dreams
I can see,
Towers and towers of books,
Fantasy, adventure, comedy too,
Not many on pirate hooks.

In my box of dreams
I can see,
Masses and masses of rabbits,
Jumping, hopping and bouncing too,
Lots having bad habits.

In my box of dreams
I can see,
Hordes and hordes of dragons,
Roaring, bellowing and growling too,
Not many in wagons.

In my box of dreams
I can see,
Groups and groups of instruments,
Pianos, trumpets, violins too,
The trumpet's being very insolent.

When I close my box of dreams
I can see,
A future full of opportunities,
With books, rabbits, dragons, instruments too,
And endless possibilities.

Anisha Zain (11)
St John's C Of E Primary School, Watford

I Wonder

I wonder why there are stars in the sky,
I wonder what makes the sky look blue,
I wonder why there is more water than land,
But the thing I wonder about most is,
What makes a dream a dream?
Why do dreams feel magical?
Why do they seem so real?
Why do you never get quite the same dream?
What makes them so scary or mystical?
When does a good dream occur?
When is it my turn to understand the universe?
Why don't we know how fast bees' wings are?
Why can't we breathe in space?
Why are there many more mysteries unsolved?
Why do people try to ignore?
Why do we have to die?
Why do we question thoughts?
How do we know what dwells in our hearts?
I wonder why dreams are dreams.

Coralie Turmaine (9)
St John's C Of E Primary School, Watford

The Colour Black

This poem is dedicated to the visually impaired people

Colour, colour, colour, oh, it's everywhere!
Green grass, blue skies and the dazzling glare,
Think of those who see black in every sphere.

"Wow! What a rainbow!" exclaims a five-year-old,
But how can I ask those,
Who cede to describe a VIBGYOR?

As the skies turn dark and gloomy,
And everyone looks frightened and panicky,
I see him walking in solitude,
Like an unstoppable bee.

He is fearless and firm in his own way,
He is not daunted by any obstacle,
That may come his way.

Disabled is not him,
who has lived his life righteous,
For so many seasons.

But the people who are blinded,
By a lack of morality,
And are virtuously weakened.

Manan Kashyap (9)
St John's C Of E Primary School, Watford

Once Upon A Time

O nce there were dancers,
N one of them had shoes,
C alley was a princess who was beautiful,
E veryone was surprised that Calley was so beautiful.

U p in the valley, Calley was dreaming of something,
P arrots and lots of birds were flying to her balcony,
O pening the door, she talked to the birds in bird language,
N one of them were sad, they were happy.

A ll of the birds were spinning around her.

T he girl was raised by the magic,
I , the writer, was shocked and amazed,
M illions of people were staring and amazed,
E nd part was so good, the birds rose and turned into dancers.

Civadanya Sivasuthan (9)
St John's C Of E Primary School, Watford

Dancing Fairies In My Dreams

D ancing fairies in my dreams,
A nd a wizard with my fear,
N ow, I wish I'd never see,
C unning dragons,
I n my mind,
N ow, I see its beautiful scales,
G reen eyes staring at me,

F airies' wings fluttering,
A iry mist fading them away,
I reful sniffs coming from afar,
R oaring is all I can hear,
I n my mind, all I see is darkness,
E very night, I come here, then
S uddenly, it fades away.

Shivanshi Yadav (10)
St John's C Of E Primary School, Watford

Imagination

I n this amazing land, I see,
M onkeys swing from tree to tree,
A ll sorts of animals, I can see,
G etting brighter, all to me.
I 'm getting tired, time to go to bed,
"N ight, everyone," and I rest my head,
A ll this time here in this land,
T ight and snug, I lay like a bug
I magination is a wonderful world,
O h, everything here has been a whirl,
"N ight, everyone." It's time to rest my head.

Abigail Christopher (9)
St John's C Of E Primary School, Watford

Dreams

In my dreams are different things,
Every single night.

Some are fun, some make me jump,
Some give me such a fright.

I once made spells with a wizard,
Their colours dull and bright.

I went flying with a unicorn,
Through the star-speckled night.

But some of my dreams are different,
They're nothing more than feelings.

At least one thing that's always true,
Is that they're nothing more than dreams.

Nancy Afua O' Sullivan (10)
St John's C Of E Primary School, Watford

The Dragons

D angerously, they hunt; but are kind and sweet when they are not.
R apidly, they fly, straight up into the sky,
A ll of the dragons are friendly and gentle,
G orgeous and elegant, they can try to be your friend,
O ut of all the dragons, which one will you pick?
N ow choose, go ahead - I choose Emerald,
S he's always been my friend.

Allegra Edy (8)
St John's C Of E Primary School, Watford

Penguins

P roper penguins love penguin school
E specially learning to read
N ight comes, they cannot sleep, they need to go to school
G oing to play with friends too
U s penguins love penguin library
I t is where you learn and read
N ight comes, they cannot sleep, they have to go to school
S chool comes, they can't wait.

Frania Oledzka (10)
St John's C Of E Primary School, Watford

Famous At Last

F amous at last, it's my time to shine,
A riana Grande is here; hip hip hooray!
M oon shines brightly like the stars
O h, at last, I am famous
U nder control, not out of control
S un rises - I'm so excited that it is time!

Amalia Rusu (10)
St John's C Of E Primary School, Watford

Bunny Race

Benji Benny Bunny
Hop, hop!
To the top
Don't go down
With a big frown
We believe in you
And you should too
We know you will finish the race
If you keep going at your own pace.

Prerana Prem (8)
St John's C Of E Primary School, Watford

A Showjumping Competition

Over each jump, we soar
A sensation I've never felt before
As my horse's hooves reach the floor
I wonder, *will I have a perfect score?*

I'm in my own space, I can't hear a sound
Not from the noisy crowd that surrounds
For the last time, my horse's hooves hit the ground
Now I feel the excitement around.

I exited the arena with haste
The question still lasts, where will I be placed?
Over the jumps, I had raced and raced
Hopefully, that effort didn't go to waste.

The speakers boomed: "So, who has won?"
"In only 57 seconds, I couldn't believe it could be done,"
That was my time, my smile beamed in the sun
I had come number one!

Christie Blair (11)
St Joseph's Primary School, Stepps

The House

It was a dream, not too long ago,
Sitting in a vintage type of living room.
A cold draught entered this massive space
With a toasty fireplace.
After some time, I stood up and left the living room.
Suddenly, a shrilling sense of coldness shot down my spine!
As I walked up the creaking stairs, I raced into a room.
This room was so different; it was more upbeat somehow.
The coldness left me, and all my fears went away.
This room was everything I'd ever dreamt.
There was another door, I ventured through.
There were my friends.
We sat and talked for hours upon hours.
Then I woke up. What just happened?

Orla Rose (12)
St Joseph's Primary School, Stepps

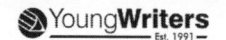

Winter

A cold night can make you shiver,
As your arms and legs begin to quiver.
As clear as day,
You hear creatures begin to say,
"It's winter, it's winter, finally."

The squirrels get the nuts,
The bears get the cones,
And the badgers get the berries.
The trees are bare as winter is in the air.
A lonesome creature has nowhere to go.
Poor creature, out there all alone.
It's cold and quiet, and holding a stick,
The creature spotted a light.
"A light, a light, I can see,
Please, someone take pity on me."

Eva-Rose Brolly
St Joseph's Primary School, Stepps

Golden Retrievers

Golden retrievers, oh so fine,
With fur as golden as sunshine,
Their tails wag with pure delight,
Bringing warmth and joy, day and night.

Their eyes so kind and full of love,
Their gentle souls from high above,
With hearts as big as can be,
They're loyal friends, you see.

Whether running through fields or by your side,
They're always there, a loyal guide,
Golden Retrievers, forever true,
In our hearts, we will cherish you.

Isla Lundie (12)
St Joseph's Primary School, Stepps

Showjumping

S oaring above jumps so high
H oping we don't knock a pole
O nwards, upwards, over we fly
W inning is our only goal
J umping over a water tray
U nder the bright blue sky
M aybe today's our lucky day
P raying time won't go by
I n sync with my horse
N ear the end of the course
G ot to get over the last fence!

Cara Malcolm-Gourley
St Joseph's Primary School, Stepps

The Scary Mare

I was watching the mare,
With its swishy golden hair.
It trotted everywhere,
Without a single care.

Suddenly, it stared me down,
From my toes to my crown.
But there was no sound,
All except hooves on the ground.

It was chasing me!
As fast as the eye could see.
Before it got me,
It all went misty.

Then I was in my bed,
On a cold January morning.

Hazel Izuagba
St Joseph's Primary School, Stepps

A Wish

I wish I was on my holidays,
With warm nights and sunny days.
If my friend was with me, it would be a blast.
For many years, a dream from my past.
During the day, we'd play in the pool,
And every day would be so cool.
Other days, we'd go to the beach to play in the sand,
Some of the adults would have a piña colada in hand.
When the holiday was over, we'd all feel upset.

Aaron Connelly (11)
St Joseph's Primary School, Stepps

Dreamers

D reams are a hope beneath our feet,
R eminding us of thoughts so deep,
E ven at night, they're the heroes amongst all,
A fter midnight, their minds so tall,
M ighty worlds jump in-between,
E normous giants, then a king or a queen,
R emember though, not every dream is alright,
S ome could even give you a terrible fright!

Liam Buckley
St Joseph's Primary School, Stepps

The Snake

One fateful night in the land of Nod,
I was chased by something slithery and odd.
Never was I prepared for this,
The snake bit after the hiss!
My leg swelled as I started to run,
The reptile had clearly won.
I screamed out in pain,
Only to learn it was all in vain.
No one heard my scream,
Thankfully, that was the end of my nightmare of a dream.

Aasiyah Raza
St Joseph's Primary School, Stepps

Outer Space

I'm in outer space,
I'm looking in a mirror and can't see my own face!
I'm in zero gravity and it's just a disgrace.
I can't feel my legs and my hands shake!
I'm in so much fear as Earth is no longer near.
I land on the moon with a thud.
I felt scared but not now this afternoon,
As I've landed on the moon!

Lucy Hutchison (12)
St Joseph's Primary School, Stepps

Cross-Country

As I ride across the fields
I see the breeze
Go through the trees
As I see the jump
Coming my way
I hold onto the reins
I don't go astray
The last jump
Will I make it by?
It is very high
Over the jump
I soar through the sky
And over the finish
After all this work
I've won the competition!

Willow Miller (12)
St Joseph's Primary School, Stepps

Once Upon A Haggis

O' haggis, neeps and tatties,
So yummy in my tummy.
Makes me burst,
Oh so good haggis,
O' sweet tatties,
O' sour neeps.
On Robert Burns Day, I feast.
On the 25th of January,
Bagpipes play all day long,
In Glasgow City.
O' haggis, neeps and tatties.

Toby Agboola
St Joseph's Primary School, Stepps

The Cup

In my dreams every night
The football pitch is in sight
I strike the ball and the commentator shouts, *"Goal!"*
As the final whistle blows, I am out of control
I lift the cup and lift it high
But as the alarm goes off, the dream goes by.

Frankie Ferry
St Joseph's Primary School, Stepps

Witches

When you're in bed, fast asleep
Witches come out and have a peep.
Casting spells on cats and dogs,
Turning bananas into hairy frogs.
When the sun comes up,
They go and hide.
So, boys and girls, listen closely,
Or you will turn into crunchy toast.

Megan Tang
St Joseph's Primary School, Stepps

Dream

D ays end in happy sleep
R ide across your adventure
E verywhere is magical
A lways be happy whenever it's good
M y dreams can be endless and take me anywhere I want to go.

Michael McKenna (12)
St Joseph's Primary School, Stepps

Chestnut Pony

When I grow up, I want to wake up on a warm summer's day,
And look out of my window and see the sun smiling.

When I grow up, I want to walk outside,
And water my flowers when they are dancing.

When I grow up, I want to see the deer prancing.

When I grow up, I want to ride my chestnut pony
Into the sunlight and the moonlight's rays.

When I grow up, I want to ride my chestnut pony
Into the forest and look into the green pond.

Me and my chestnut pony are a team,
We are never mean.
My chestnut pony is as red as an autumn leaf.

When I grow up, I want to gallop across the mud,
Into the fields.

When I grow up, I want to live in the countryside,
And complete my dreams with my chestnut pony.

Nia Wood (11)
Swaffham CE Junior Academy, Swaffham

I Live In Space

I live in space, my only friends are aliens and stars.
I live in space, all I do is fall around.
I live in space, when I left Earth, I waved bye,
As the Earth smiled for a while.
When I left Earth, everything changed,
It made the years longer.
When I left Earth, it was strange,
The years were longer
And I no longer knew what day it was.
When I first came here, it was weird,
Until I met a star; he was my best friend.
He always laughed at my jokes
Until one day, he just faltered away.
I was sad that one day until I met my new friend,
His name was Danny.
I could always talk to him,
He was really nice to me,
And before me, he had no one to go and see.
After we had explored the moon,
We decided to leave soon.
Maybe we could visit Saturn or Neptune.
Neptune was our choice,
So we decided to visit Neptune.

As we waved to Neptune, he waved back,
But we noticed a shiny thing on his back.
It was big, blue and beautiful.
I had never been there before,
So it was time to explore.
But first, I needed to know what that shiny thing was.
As I approached, I realised it was my old friend, Star!
I was so happy!
So he explored with us. It was so fun!
But when the day came to an end,
We would need somewhere to rest,
So we went to a building.
But soon, it got boring, so we went surfing.
Soon, this will be continued,
But for now, goodbye my new friend!

Evie Denman (11)
Swaffham CE Junior Academy, Swaffham

The Strongest Frost Dragon

One day, I travelled to Antarctica.
I said to the security guard, "May I pass?"
"You may," he said.
When I got there,
The mountains were as cold as a pile of ice cubes.
I went searching and found a massive hole.
I thought to myself, *should I do it?*
I jumped in and it sent me to this place.
I saw a llama eating a banana.
But a mythical frost dragon came,
Flying as fast as the Flash,
And sprayed his powerful frost breath at the banana.
It hit the floor and went... *Crack!*
The frost dragon sat on my shoulder,
And I sat on a chair that had a cup holder.
After sitting down, we looked around for more animals.
I found a polar bear drinking a slurpy,
And all I could hear was the polar bear going...
Slurp! Slurp!
This felt like my imagination,
So, in my mind, I thought about my dream house.
Hmmm! Oh, I know!
My door was made of iron,

My roof was made of metal that you couldn't break,
And the walls were made of diamonds,
With a free McDonald's next to the front door.
And it happened!
What a surprise!
Me and the dragon lived there for the rest of our lives.

Arnie Ward (10)
Swaffham CE Junior Academy, Swaffham

A Disney And Pixar Adventure

I could see a mystery drink on the table,
It was so tempting to try,
Just a sip,
Just one...
I got teleported to a castle,
I looked out of the window,
The trees were dancing in the distance.

I heard a quack,
It was Donald Duck,
But he was covered in muck.
Someone took his hat,
But he couldn't get it back.
Me and Donald ran outside,
And I saw lots of Disney and Pixar characters.

I stood still,
But would I find a friend?
I need to get out of here.
There was a piece of paper on the floor,
It said: 'Go to the one who lost a shoe'.
I walked into the Pixar section and I saw a sign,

That read: 'Disney princesses',
So I went there,
I couldn't bear.
There was Elsa,
There was Ariel,
And Cinderella,
She was the one who lost her shoe.

She said to me,
"I think this must be."
She handed me a note,
Or was it a quote?

It read: 'Go back to the start and bring along a friend,
This has been fun'.

I thought to myself,
I should stay here,
And it is better here.

Jessica Smith (10)
Swaffham CE Junior Academy, Swaffham

My Worst Nightmare

My nightmare is scary, *bang!*
That's what I call it rarely.
I run and I run
Until I see something that comes to a stop.
I can only see smoke,
Please tell me this is a joke!
My nightmare is about me getting lost,
Just before this, I was eating candyfloss.
The tree has hands that are trying to grab me,
Little do I know, someone is behind me.
I step on a spider,
Since then, I've forgotten that I am alone,
Hopefully, someone will come and take me home.
Can I just admire it,
And not see a pirate?
This isn't up to me,
Oh no, maybe not.
It is a clown with a frown,
It is left and right,
Everywhere I look, it is there.
I run and run,
And notice the clown is getting mad.
I climb up a tree,

Hoping it isn't following me,
I look behind me,
Oh gosh, it is there.
Suddenly, at that moment,
I woke up wondering what was there.

Neila Moura (10)
Swaffham CE Junior Academy, Swaffham

Flying Atop A Dragon

I go to sleep and rest my head,
But when I wake up,
I'm not in my bed.
I stand up and walk around,
Until I find out,
That I'm above the ground!
I walk around some more,
Placing my feet
Upon the floor.
I find that I'm on a ship,
Atop a dragon.
I walk to the upper deck,
When I feel a hand
Grab my neck.
I turn around
And there's a jolly-looking man.
He asks me what I'm doing here,
And I tell him,
"I have no idea."
He says that his name's Slate
And he places people's dinner
Upon their plate,
For he is the cook of this crew.

He introduces me to the rest of the crew,
And the dragon,
She's named Shrew.
We go on many adventures through the land
Until I wake up
And my life is once again bland.

Jensen Frost (10)
Swaffham CE Junior Academy, Swaffham

Crikey!

Me and Gabe were in the Outback,
We were walking and heard a crack.
I turned around and saw a herd of kangaroos,
They showed us their funky moves.

We kept on walking in the Outback,
Then we heard a crack.
We looked up and saw a koala,
He told us he wanted to go to Guatemala.

We kept on walking in the Outback until we crashed,
Into a river, then the river splashed.
We looked and saw a saltwater crocodile,
He made us run a mile.

We kept on walking in the Outback,
Then we heard a crack.
We looked at the tree and saw a frilled-neck lizard,
It showed us its frill and said it wanted to see a blizzard.

We kept on walking in the Outback,
Then we heard a crack.

It was a snake called Mikey,
And he said, "*Crikey!*"

Dougie Lawes (11)
Swaffham CE Junior Academy, Swaffham

Enchanted Secrets Behind A Forest

Trees are big, animals are small,
I have a home but it's not for all.
There might be a secret,
But it's not an excuse.
"A fake wall," you say.
"I wonder why?" you say.
Drop! Drop! Drop!
Plop! Plop! Plop!
Crack!
A big gush of water as it comes out,
No one knows where it's come from.
"Beautiful waterfall," I hear you say.
"Can I go through you?" I say.
As I wander over there,
I find a portal and then I stare.
I think, *should I go through or not?*
Is there a good reason why I cannot?
As I stand in the portal,
I doubt, *should I have done this,*
Or will I regret it all?

Charlotte Chasney (10)
Swaffham CE Junior Academy, Swaffham

Firefighters

Red and gold flames glistening
In the reflection of my eyes.
The screams of families,
The fear in little kids' lives,
Wood screaming for help,
As the fire burns it carelessly.

Firefighters charge into buildings,
Like warriors on the battlefield,
Firefighters risk their lives to save someone else's.

Firefighters are real superheroes,
Without them, our world would be dust.
It's my dream to become one,
To become someone who saves people's lives each day.
Maybe that dream will come true someday.

Firefighters inspire me,
Firefighters encourage me,
A firefighter is what I want to be,
Firefighters are my once upon a dream.

Lottie Cope (10)
Swaffham CE Junior Academy, Swaffham

George The Crazy Monkey

I was walking through the emerald-green woods,
I saw a monkey whispering to me,
And he said, "My name is George,
And I like being very loud."
The monkey could swing from tree to tree,
He liked eating whipped cream.
He went to get me some Ribena,
And he loved drinking it with me.

He swung from tree to tree,
To show his friends his whipped cream.
George took me to his house,
Which was made out of whipped cream.
Then he showed me his schemes,
Then took me to his room full of ice cream.
He fed me some of his strawberry ice cream,
With a class of Ribena.

Tommy Patrick (11)
Swaffham CE Junior Academy, Swaffham

Imagination

Have you ever been lost in imagination,
Where you can be anything you want,
If you haven't, let me help.
In your imagination, you can be a fairy,
Or you can be very, very scary.
You can be a wizard,
Or a snow monster caught in a blizzard.

A place where anything can happen,
Where you can fly,
Or be a clown
And only eat pie.
Or you can go to space
As an astronaut,
At a rapid pace,

A place where you can write,
Or get into a fight,
With a dragon or a dinosaur.
You can be famous,
Or anything you want,
Follow your imagination.

Rosie Askew (10)
Swaffham CE Junior Academy, Swaffham

Fly With Me

As I live on the ground, I run around,
Looking up, wishing for luck,
A wild horse just bucked.
I need luck living in the ground,
At least I can run around.
May I lie or may I fly,
One more time, just like old times?
Can the skies be mine once again?
As I run, thinking of fun,
I leap into the sky and fly.
As I whoosh along the trees,
I can finally see what it means to break free,
As I soar through the air, I just don't care.
And now I am free,
So I can finally be the real me.

Gabriel Gomes (11)
Swaffham CE Junior Academy, Swaffham

Future

F uture is coming as quickly as a light switch
U nited, you and I can make a difference
T herefore, we will make a big difference
U sing all of our thoughts
R ainforests being chopped down
E veryone will make a big difference, a big difference.

Charlie Smith (10)
Swaffham CE Junior Academy, Swaffham

Footballer

Imagine you are a footballer,
And you get to play with your idol.
Both of you get a Ballon d'Or,
Both of you don't play for the same nation,
And then you play against each other.
Later, in that same game,
It is half-time,
And it's 1-0 to your idol...

Aiden Nash-Choppen (10)
Swaffham CE Junior Academy, Swaffham

The Dragon Explorer

I woke up in a bed,
I went out of my home
And out there,
Dragons were dancing in the air,
So I climbed onto the roof
And leapt like a frog
Onto a dragon
To explore other islands,
To find...
Treasures
And different species
Of dragon!

Oliver Starr (10)
Swaffham CE Junior Academy, Swaffham

I Am Harry Potter

I have a scar,
But I don't drive a car.
I have a friend called Ron,
No, it is not a con.
I have a boss called Dumbledore,
But he can fit through a single door.
I go down to the lobby,
To meet my friend, Dobby,
Then we go on a jolly.

Harry Todd (10)
Swaffham CE Junior Academy, Swaffham

Lyle The Crocodile

Lyle was a crocodile,
While he was bored, he ran a mile.
Lyle was a kind type of crocodile,
While his friends were at home playing games,
He ran a mile.

Craig Russell (10)
Swaffham CE Junior Academy, Swaffham

The Clown

It was 1am on a gloomy Tuesday morning,
I was finishing off a poster for my homework about the planet.
I had finally finished after hours on end,
I started walking upstairs to my bed
I went up and up.

Just as I was walking up the spiralling stairs,
I heard the door handle rattling.
Rattle, rattle, and *rattle*
I ran to my room, shut the door
It was a haunting sound I had never heard before!
I hid under my blanket.
Out of the corner of my eye, I saw a red ball floating in the air
I realised it looked like a clown out of a fair!
It came into my dark room and switched on my light
I feared for my life.
The clown looked like he wanted to play,
A game of hide-and-seek - I tried to run away.

My legs turned to lead,
He chuckled like a hyena.

He vanished from sight; I heard his laugh in the attic.
Thuds above me, I panicked.

I knew I had to somehow fight.
I grabbed my trusty bat
My dad bought me from a baseball game
I had to be brave.

The clown appeared once again,
He sniggered and cackled at my windowpane
Something felt sharp, a pinch in my chest.
Suddenly, I blacked out; was it poison?

I woke up in an abandoned clown house.
I heard a *ping*,
I ran at full speed through the mirror room,
I almost splattered into a mirror.
Mirror, mirror, mirror.
It was endless.

As I stopped, I turned around to see,
Hundreds of clowns gazing at me.
I ran through a door only to be met with a room full of fire.
It was like hell!
Eerie creatures filled the room,
I felt a presence glaring at me.

As I turned around, a wolf looking thing with bat wings screeched,
And flew at me,
In the blink of an eye.
I ran with all my might, I came to a halt,
At a crack in the floor
I had to be daring, to a fault.

I leapt for my life over the six-foot-long gap,
My leg hit the other side of the crack,
Blood poured out.

The wolf picked me up in its mouth and flew me up to its nest.
Where they feasted on me, my body and the rest.

Suddenly, I woke up in my own bed; was this a dream?
I heard a whispering scream...

D Hanlon (12)
The Kibworth Mead Academy, Kibworth Beauchamp

Magical Fairy Party

I walk through this dark forest,
It's a little scary if I'm honest.
Pixies fly gently in the air,
A gentle breeze rushes through my hair.

Mushrooms glow in the night,
In-between the trees are spots of moonlight.
The stream glitters in the light of the moon,
It will be time for the Queen's palace party soon.

I've arrived just in time,
I can see all the guests queuing in line.
The queen fairy is wearing her shiny crown,
She looks so elegant in her brilliant blue ball gown.
I am ready to dance into the night,
It's so exciting to party tonight.

When I was dancing, I needed a break,
Then I went to the buffet to get a piece of cake.
When I'd finished, I looked at the clock,
Having to go home was such a shock.
The ballroom was now shut,
So off I went back to my toadstool hut.

Primrose Worsdale-Mann (10)
The Meadows Primary School, Lincoln

Pokémon

In a world of wonder where creatures roam,
A magical land of adventure, a place to call home.
Where Pikachu and Charmander, side by side,
Embark on quests and reach for the sky.

Their hearts full of courage, their spirits pure,
Their bond with their trainers, a bond like no other.
Through forests of grass and mountains so high,
They journey on with a spirit that never dies.

Their battles fierce, their triumphs sweet,
Their dreams of victory, a treasure to keep.
With each catch, their strength grows,
Their legendary powers for all to know.

Their roars echo through the land,
Their hearts full of fire, their souls grand.
In this world of Pokémon, they thrive,
A never-ending journey, a life to survive.

Barry Winter (9)
The Meadows Primary School, Lincoln

I Want A Snow Day On My Birthday!

Spring, summer, autumn and winter, we have the lot,
But I dream of snow in the flowerpots.
I've been to the Falkland Islands where I experienced four seasons in one day,
But I dream of snow, playing all day.

In the spring, lambs are born,
But I dream of snow on top of the fields filled with corn.
In the autumn, I cycle on the crispy leaves,
But I dream of snow in the springtime eaves.

In Antarctica, it snows all day and the bears love to play,
But I dream of snow in the spring every day.
The reason I dream of snow all the time,
Is because the twenty-eighth of March is my important day.

So I dream of a day where I have snow on my birthday!

Sienna Webber (10)
The Meadows Primary School, Lincoln

My Not So Dreams

It's not always easy for me at night
To get to sleep when off goes my light
Because some of my dreams are bad
I get visited by scary beasts that make me sad

Some are well-known, like scary clowns in disguise
The others are unknown creepy creatures that tell me lies
Sometimes they visit me in a tall, dark and mysterious forest
With trees that have long and rugged arms to curl around my chest

But that's the thing with sleep and dreams
They don't allow you to control what you see
I prefer the ones with my friend, Harry Potter
Where my dad's a wizard and there's no scary beasts to bother.

Cohen Tostevin (10)
The Meadows Primary School, Lincoln

The Dreamer

The dreamer dreams of a wonderful day,
Where everyone shuts up and gets on their way.

The dreamer dreams of a wonderful land,
Where wizards and witches are roaming hand in hand.

The dreamer dreams of *no* school at all,
Just a world full of tech and muddy rugby balls.

The dreamer dreams of a perfect meal,
With candy galore, what a tremendous deal!

The dreamer dreams of fluffy pandas who are red,
They become best friends and he names one Ed.

The dreamer dreams of fierce lightsaber duels,
But look! He's woken up and it's time for school.

Isaac Everson (10)
The Meadows Primary School, Lincoln

Her Flying Fish

One day, a girl lay in bed dreaming about her fish flying in the night sky,
She zoomed up, up, up into the night.
Up above the puffy clouds into space, she flew,
Until they landed on the moon.
Where she met a friend or two,
They were aliens; one green, one blue
Together, they tried moon rock stew!
Until at last she said, "I have to go back to my mum and dad."
She said goodbye to her alien friends, got on her fish and off they flew,
Back to Earth and into bed.
She never forgot the adventure she had,
With her flying fish and her alien friends.

Jessica Cooper (10)
The Meadows Primary School, Lincoln

My Cat, Bailey

I had a cat called Bailey,
Who used to follow me around daily.

He was black, white and brown,
Our furry king without a crown.

When my mum gave him food,
It always put him in a good mood.

He liked to sit on my dad's knee,
I wish he'd come and sit with me.

When I miss him and feel like I want to cry,
I look up and know he's now the brightest star in the sky.

Isabelle Onyon (9)
The Meadows Primary School, Lincoln

Hidden Dreams

D elightful dreams make you smile
R eally hilarious dreams make you laugh
E xciting stories make you want to find out more
A mazing dreams fill your heart
M ysterious imaginary lands let you do whatever you feel
S cary dreams make you want to open your eyes.

Wake up!

Elisabeth Corson (10)
The Meadows Primary School, Lincoln

The Space Wonder World

The moonlight shines,
The galaxy roars,
The spacemen are coming,
Out of Mars,
Space shuttles and aliens are trying to float about,
But the atmosphere won't let them out,
I heard a mighty bang,
Then my 7am alarm rang.

Joel Hirons (10)
The Meadows Primary School, Lincoln

The Monster

I lay in bed, tossing and turning, trying to get to sleep,
I take a drink and hope to doze off while I weep.
I finally get under my blanket and close my eyes,
Yay, finally God answered my cries.
I teleported into a forest with trees surrounding me in every direction,
I tried grabbing my phone that was in my pocket but there was no connection.
I heard footsteps sounding faster and faster,
I screeched and ran whilst hearing, "Hi, master."
I ran and ran and cut myself on a branch; oh no, I need a plaster.
I sprinted like a wolf chasing its prey,
I wish I was in a restaurant getting served food on a tray.
I looked behind me and saw a furry monster running towards me,
While I was running, my sight was trees that I could see.
I ran and ran until I saw an old cabin,
On top of the cabin was a bird that was a robin.
I knocked on the crusty old door, waiting for someone to open it,
I looked in the window to see a woman hit.

She opened the door as I stood,
Leaning against the wood.
She said nothing as I was in a hurry,
She let me inside as I was worried.
I asked the woman if she could help me with the fluffy, gigantic, evil, red-eyed monster,
She said she wouldn't mind helping me if I drank the potion.
I gulped it down and started to turn taller,
I started hitting the monster and beating it.
The monster flew and said, "Hey, look up!"
He flew down and landed on me,
I couldn't breathe since the monster sat on me.
My muscles started to fade away,
And that's when I heard the monster say,
"Wake up, wake up, wake up!"
And that's when I woke up in my comfy bed,
Under my fluffy blanket.

Poppy A (10)
The St Margaret's CE Primary School, Withern

The Unknown Dimension

There I lay in my warm comfy bed,
While wondrous ideas run through my head.
My eyes are sleepy, I'm dozing away,
Reliving the stories from my eventful day.
Then *whoosh!* My eyes open once more,
And I can no longer see the floor.
All but myself has vanished now,
I stay as calm as my thoughts allow.
Something has scrambled across the ground,
Making a rather frightening sound.
As the creature whispers in the dark,
I see a blinding, fiery spark.
It hurts my eyes, I squeeze them shut,
Is it a monster or a power cut?
I blink three times, then a 4th and 5th,
Is it the bulb or a reborn myth?
Click! The light slowly rises high,
I shout, "Come on out! Don't be shy!"
With a meow and a swish of her tail,
She leaps to the door, determined to bail.
I see her silhouette, we come face to face,
I hold her tight with a relieved embrace.
It's my cat, Tips, no monster at all,

As fast as a bullet, she shoots down the hall.
I made a mistake, her hiss like a whisper,
But also another, my cat is a *mister!*

Camilla E (10)
The St Margaret's CE Primary School, Withern

Mischievous Pirate

M ischievously, he stole some treasure,
I f there wasn't any treasure, he would be sad
S cratching his head, he had a vital idea,
C autiously, he tried to get on the boat,
H eavily breathing, he got on the boat,
I f he didn't know they were on board, he would be caught
E ven though they were on there, he hopped on,
V ery fast, he ran from deck to deck,
O n board, it was very rough,
U nder the quarter especially
S uspiciously, he hid, so nobody could see him.

P assing everyone on board, he got to the treasure,
I nterestingly, there was stuff that wasn't for pirates,
R ating every item from one to ten,
A t that moment, he was rating everything six,
T here was stuff on there that was fascinating,
E verything was the best that he saw.

Freddie Howell (9)
The St Margaret's CE Primary School, Withern

Clowns In The Darkness

C reepin' behind your back
L urks the mysterious clowns
O pening their mouths wide
W anting to take a bite
N ever turning around
S cared to take a look

I n the gloomy darkness
N o one is in the room to help

T hud! Something around me moves
H iding under the bed, clowns jump out
E very clown stares deep into my terrified eyes

D angling from the ceiling
A re sticky, silver cobwebs
R ubbing my hands to keep warm
K eeping extremely quiet
N o sound to be heard
E ntering the dusty corner
S ulking in the room
S uddenly, I'm safe at home in my own bed.

Sienna D (10)
The St Margaret's CE Primary School, Withern

Stranger And Stranger

Sleepily, I awake,
Looking down, I see my dog shake,
Then float up in the air,
All I can do is stare,
Like I am not even aware.

My curtains open by themselves,
And my books hop off all the shelves,
Then out of the blue, I see,
Something that belongs in the sea,
It really is quite a strange thing,
A whale flapping its single wing.

My eyes open wider and wider,
As my bed starts floating higher,
I feel quite light myself,
And I worry about my health,

Stranger, this world becomes,
From my pillows, I hear hums,
My clothes start to sing,
My ears begin to ring,
Then, all goes black,
I wake up with a whack,

My brother is staring down at me,
He screams in my face, "It's time for tea!"

Skye L (11)
The St Margaret's CE Primary School, Withern

The Night Of One Million

Lost in the mysterious woods,
Crunching leaves everywhere.
Hearing loud and crashing thuds,
Spiders crawling in my hair.

Following me close behind,
Oscar the cat is crawling.
Keeping me company, you will find,
Stopping me from stalling.

Suddenly, from in a bush,
Rustling could be heard,
I trotted along in a rush,
I hoped it was a bird.

Surprisingly, it was not what I thought,
It seemed to be gentle and kind,
I should probably look, I think I ought,
One million cats dash out in the wind!

Nixi H (9)
The St Margaret's CE Primary School, Withern

Dancing Dreams

D ancing on the stage
A nd feeling scared
N ever give up
'C ause tonight's the night I win
I magining I'm with a team
N ear the end, it gives me confidence
G iving me a medal

D oing the performance made me happy
R eminding me of how lucky I am
E veryone looking at me
A mazing things happen when you try
M e, buoyant after my dance
S miling as bright as the stars; suddenly, I realise it's a dream.

Skylar Greasley (9)
The St Margaret's CE Primary School, Withern

Midnight Magic

In my dreams, every night,
I always see the sky so bright.
There I lay on the floor,
Thinking, *should I open the door?*
I decide to open it into the dream,
Leading me to my doom so clean.
I see spiders and stars, trees and all,
Then I find myself about to fall.
But when I see a dragon nearby,
I suddenly realise I'm about to fly.
As I soar up into the air,
I see unicorns flicking their hair.
As I wake up, I see I'm home,
And on my table, I see a comb.

Alice W (8)
The St Margaret's CE Primary School, Withern

Unknown

U nknown surroundings with the darkness around,
N othing in the blackness but me and Faith,
K nowing nothing but us and angel statues,
N ow, as we blink, the statues move closer,
O nly inches away from us with outstretched hands,
W e run away with the angel close behind,
N ow it is here, we close our eyes, then we wake.

Zara L G (10)
The St Margaret's CE Primary School, Withern

Strange World

I am sleeping amongst the stars,
Tasting yummy chocolate bars.
When suddenly, I feel a log hit my head
And see things I've only read.
I've got superpowers,
It's been an hour,
I'm now lying down in a tower.
I think I'm in jail,
My face has gone pale.
I see a monster,
Called Oompa Loompa.
Then I see a key,
Under my knee.
It's been a decade,
The key breaks.
I see a twig,
And I think of a pig.
Everyone starts to say,
"Please help us!" in a type of way.
"Please save our world,
The pearl is lost,
Taken by Jack Frost!"
I get out of jail,

I find a nail.
"It's red," a voice said.
"Who are you?
Where are you?
How do you do?"
"None of us are brave,
We found this nail in a cave."
So I put it in the right place,
At a really slow pace.
I find a pea that is green,
I eat it and become a queen,
Now I am back in my bed,
And nothing comes to my head.

Anaisha Rathi (8)
Ursuline Preparatory School, Warley

Getting Lost

"Go to bed," Mum said.
"Go to sleep, my sleepy head."
So I went to bed and I had a dream,
And on the way, I met a frog,
And he said, "I'm not a log."

So I walked along,
And on the way, I met a cat.
"Look, I met a bat."
And then I met a little monkey,
"Oh my gosh, the tracks look bumpy."

And on the way, I met a sheep.
"Sheesh, you've got to look neat."
And then I met a little dog.
"Can you just fetch me that log, for Frog?"

And then I met a monster.
"Arghhh!"
And the monster said,
"You're going really red."

And then I met a unicorn,
She saved me from this scary dream.

I thought she kicked my head,
But my mum just stroked my little head!
And then I woke up in my bed.

Jessica Spilkin (7)
Ursuline Preparatory School, Warley

P-Oh-Em

I had a dream, you should know,
It was silly, I know,
I used my imagination, bro,
I thought of it, head to toe.

I was fighting a foe,
I saw extinct animals, like a dodo,
They came to life and said, "Hello,"
I asked them why they had to go.

We should keep this planet just so,
Like it was years ago,
Something happened, oh no,
And so I ran, "Got to go."

I woke up in my bed,
And off to school I go,
About this dream, I should show,
We should change the planet,
Like a superhero.

Oliver Browne (8)
Ursuline Preparatory School, Warley

Dancing Fairies

Dancing fairies are so, so cool
And they all rule
They are exceptionally small
And they are very good at April Fool's
Although they can be good
Sometimes, they do not do what they should

Tonight, the fairies are doing a fairy dance
You can see them if you get the chance
When the fairies' song goes wrong
They stop singing their fairy song

So if you see them in your dream
In your nightmares, they'll always scream
So watch out for the fairy dance,
And run away... if you get the chance.

Ariana Wiggett (8)
Ursuline Preparatory School, Warley

Being Famous

Being famous is a nightmare
On the red carpet; *flash, flash* everywhere
Cameras, cameras everywhere
"Stand here, stand there,"
Says the paparazzi over there
This isn't a dream, it is a nightmare!

The red carpet is tearing
And nobody is caring
They are all preparing
For the special ending

And now, I am sending myself back awake
And now, my life is not at stake
I am safe and sound back in my bed
And then my mother said,
"Go back to bed!" Oh no!

Arabella George (8)
Ursuline Preparatory School, Warley

The Space Monster

I'm going to bed
And I wish I said
That I can stay awake instead
I started to dream
You shouldn't know what I've seen
I hear scratching and patching all over the place
And now I see a monster lurking in space
Now, I am scared
So unprepared
To face the monster right in space
Now, I'm running all over the place
You should have seen his scary face
Now, it is morning
I still hear the roaring
But now, I wake up and I am safe and sound.

Katerina Stowe-Mici (8)
Ursuline Preparatory School, Warley

Superpower Football

F ootwork quicker than the Flash
O ffside rule (unless you're cool)
O verhead throw with the strength of Superman
T ricks like headers or laser vision
B icycle kicks and backflips like Spider-Man
A mazing players with superpower skills
L ionel Messi has the skills like Iron Man
L ooping a ball into the goal!

Awesome football!

Ranveer Sandhu (7)
Ursuline Preparatory School, Warley

YOUNG WRITERS INFORMATION

We hope you have enjoyed reading this book – and that you will continue to in the coming years.

If you're a young writer who enjoys reading and creative writing, or the parent of an enthusiastic poet or story writer, do visit our website **www.youngwriters.co.uk**. Here you will find free competitions, workshops and games, as well as recommended reads, a poetry glossary and our blog.

If you would like to order further copies of this book, or any of our other titles, then please give us a call or visit **www.youngwriters.co.uk**.

Young Writers
Remus House
Coltsfoot Drive
Peterborough
PE2 9BF
(01733) 890066
info@youngwriters.co.uk

YoungWritersUK **YoungWritersCW**
youngwriterscw **youngwriterscw**